Thinking for the Day

A COMPILATION OF
JOHN DENNEY'S
THOUGHTS FOR THE DAY
ORIGINALLY BROADCAST ON
BBC RADIO LEICESTER

VOL. 1

Cover photograph by author: *The Thinker* by Auguste Rodin, at National Museum of Western Art (Kokuritsu Seiyō Bijutsukan), Ueno Park, Tokyo.

Other illustrations or photographs are either the author's own, public domain or ©Valerie Denney 2011.

Published 2011

Radiance Press

35 Laurel Road, Blaby, Leicester LE8 4DL, England

Biblical quotations are taken from various translations of the bible, and are used in accordance with their respective copyright licenses. The copyright notices of the versions are:

Did you ever stop to think, and forget to start again?

Winnie the Pooh

TABLE OF CONTENTS

FOREWORD

Some time in the early 1990s, Rev. John Rackley, minister of Stoneygate Baptist Church in Leicester, and then Religious Affairs Producer for BBC Radio Leicester[1], asked me to join a rota of Sunday newspaper reviewers on the *Christian Programme*. It involved getting to the studio for 7.00 am (everything I do for BBC Radio Leicester involves getting up at a ridiculous hour!), reading through the Sunday Papers, and delivering a four-minute review. Some time later, John was called to pursue his ministry in the ancient city of Bath, and I was inherited by his successor as producer, Sandra Herbert.

Sandra persevered with me, and even arranged for me to do a little reporting for the programme, having taught me all about editing ¼" recording tape with yellow wax pencil, razor blade and sticky tape. Nowadays they do it with advanced digital computer technology, which is much better. But every technological improvement is also a little loss. Once, I understood side-valve car engines, but modern cars don't even have carburettors whose needles I used to be able to unclog. And I was a dab hand at changing those red-and-black typewriter ribbons. Another thing, schools don't even have ink monitors these days. But I digress …..

Some time in the mid 1990s, Sandra asked if I would like to contribute to the Monday to Friday *Thought for the*

---

[1] On 104.9 FM, DAB and on the BBC iPlayer website: http://www.bbc.co.uk/iplayer/console/bbc_radio_leicester

Day slot. I wrote and pre-recorded the first few of my *Thoughts* and then was invited to become one of the privileged live Thinkers.

Sandra's brief was clear: be interesting; bring a Christian perspective to topical events[2]; don't be preachy; and above all, do not exceed two minutes fifteen seconds. In the early years of the 21st century under a new producer, Chris Highton, the time was further reduced to ninety seconds – about 260 words at my speed of delivery. It's tough achieving all these goals in such a compact format!

How well I succeeded is for you to judge. Here is a collection of the earliest fifty *Thoughts* I have on record. The palaeolithic *oeuvre* was lost when we said goodbye to our Amstrad Computer[3] with its bizarre 3-inch disks in 1998. So this volume spans August 1998 to February 2003. I've presumptuously stated that this is volume 1 of a series. If you like it, I could put two or three later ones together. Let me know.

Wherever necessary, I've included, as footnotes, something of the topical background that I brought my limited brainpower to. It's surprising how some hot and vital issue fades from the memory within a very few years. So perhaps this is also a trip down Memory Lane for you and me both.

---

[2] Most of these are live scripts, but a few are from pre-recorded scripts of a more generic character.

[3] An Amstrad PCW8256, running Locoscript word processing software.

A number of the illustrations in this book are by my talented wife, Val, who has put up with my alarm going off at 05:45 at least once a month for the last fifteen years or so.

It has been a privilege to bring a Christian perspective on events to some tens of thousands of Leicestershire people. I hope it has been a gentle perspective, but I also hope that some people have at least thought, "Hmm! That's an interesting way of looking at things. I didn't know Christians thought like that." And maybe *they* have been prompted to have a *Thought for the Day* for themselves.

I apologise to the theologians among my listeners and readers: the *Thoughts* are not a vehicle for fine points of academic debate. I don't think I've strayed far from the mainstream of Christian thought and practice. But do *Think* for yourself! Please feel free to disagree with my thinking: I make no claim to infallibility!

If humour in the Christian context offends you, then you might find my occasional jokes tiresome. If so, I'm sorry. For you. God has a sense of humour, else He wouldn't have created me - or you! And, if you spot an infelicitous phrase or two, please remember that the rhetorical devices I have used here and there are for the spoken word, not necessarily the written word. And broadcasting is a spoken format.

Nor are the *Thoughts* intended to convert anyone. They "do what it says on the tin": they are a simple thought that might help people to understand a little of God's message and plan for mankind, and maybe live a little closer to His way.   **John Denney**   November 2011

My first Thought for each day .....

Now, where did I leave my trousers?

WORDS

Friday 14 August 1998

It was a bit of a *barnburner*, yesterday. All those *saddoes* – you know, the *mouse potatoes*, the *hippy dippies*, everyone who's *off message* – well, 2000 of them got into the new Oxford English dictionary. If you didn't know, a barnburner is an exciting event, a saddo is someone with a pitiable life, a mouse potato is someone who spends too long sitting at his computer[4], a hippy dippy is someone whose lifestyle is well-meaning but chaotic, and being off message means you're not toeing the party line[5].

And the dictionary, which, after all, is just a list of words available for use, simply records the glorious way the English language changes over time. It's one of the reasons that English is spoken as a first or second language by more people than any other is, and why that number is increasing all the time. Mind you, there's English and then there's English! In Pidgin, the dialect of English spoken in Papua New Guinea, they have a wonderful word: see if you can guess what it means: **Himbigfellayouhitiminiteefhesing**. No? It's a piano. And if you hit him in the teeth, he sure sings!

---

[4] e.g. me.

[5] The *Labour* Party line – Prime Minister Tony Blair was very concerned that all his Parliamentary troops stuck closely to what "Project New Labour" was about. He had spoken about toeing the party line the previous weekend.

1

And there are dangerous differences between English English and American English. Americans wear their vest over their shirt, and we wear them under. Their *pants* and *knickers* are respectable outer garments, and ours aren't.

Words are important. They describe things and define them and help us communicate with each other. The Bible sometimes calls Jesus **The Word**. That's because He is the description of God, the definition of God, and the way in which God communicates with us. And, so we can understand it, the language of the Bible has to be updated afresh for each new generation in this fast-changing world. Most of us struggle with the nearly 400-year old King James translation of the Bible. But new words and new grammar don't change the meaning. Here's something from the opening of John's gospel in a very new translation:

> *The Word was first, the Word present to God, God present to the Word. The Word was God ...The Word became flesh and blood, and moved into the neighbourhood*[6].

And surely, the arrival of the Almighty to live amongst us is the biggest barnburner of all time! The trouble is ... so many of us have gone off message!

---

[6] John 1:1-2a,14 MSG

FORGIVENESS

MONDAY 14 SEPTEMBER 1998

I've been reading a lot about someone recently.

Guess who!

He started life in a poor family in an obscure and unimportant region of his country. Younger than most who reached his position, he became Commander-in-chief of his country's armies, and went on to win a war against a dangerous power in the Middle East. In his leisure time, he was something of a musician. He was a very successful politician, and made policies and laws which brought great prosperity to his people. He brought in a "three strikes and you're out" law, which gave his people confidence that criminals would be brought to justice.

There was a down side to this great success, however. This otherwise great man had a weakness. He had a succession of mistresses and got into a lot of trouble over one of them in particular. His sexual misdeeds became the subject of scandal and caused some people to call for his resignation. He lied about his sordid behaviour, but eventually things got so bad that he repented in public for his misdeeds.

Well, I guess you realise that I'm talking about ..... King David, the King that the Jews look back to as the establisher of their kingdom. Despite all his wrongdoing, particularly in arranging for the husband of a woman he lusted after to be killed in battle, he came to represent a kingly ideal. The Israelites forgave King David and went on to regard him as one of the greatest Jews of all time. They saw in him many of the qualities they believed their Messiah would have.

Christians believe that Jesus was the Messiah that the Jews were looking for. And Jesus had something to say about sexual misconduct. Some Jewish leaders wanted to stone a woman caught in the act of adultery to death. Jesus told them

> The sinless one among you, go first: Throw the stone."
> ... Hearing that, they walked away, one after another,
> beginning with the oldest. The woman was left alone.
> Jesus stood up and spoke to her. "Woman, where are
> they? Does no one condemn you?" "No one, Master."
> "Neither do I," said Jesus. "Go on your way. From
> now on, don't sin."[7]

President Clinton has asked for forgiveness for his grubby conduct[8]. It remains to be seen whether the American people will forgive him for betraying the high ideals of his office.

But perhaps *we* might start forgiving those who have sinned against us, not because they deserve it, but because we are all sinners too.

---

[7] John 8:7-11 MSG

[8] US President Bill Clinton had recently been exposed in a sordid sexual scandal with a young White House intern, Monica Lewinski. He was impeached by the Senate but acquitted. However, he later confessed to sexual misconduct with her.

THE PAST CATCHES UP
FRIDAY 23 OCTOBER 1998

So, General Pinochet, the former dictator of Chile, over here for medical treatment, has been arrested on a Spanish extradition warrant. It's alleged that he masterminded some atrocious crimes of torture and murder twenty years or so ago. It's clear his supporters didn't expect him to be arrested after all this time.

With Martin O'Neill staying as Leicester City's manager[9], I guess many supporters have been cracking a bottle or two of champagne to celebrate. But perhaps not a bottle of the 1907 vintage Bubbly brought up from the cold, dark, bottom of the Baltic Sea. It was part of the cargo of a ship sunk by a German submarine in 1916. Mind you, a single bottle of it has just been auctioned for £2,400, so small glasses are in order! They say it hasn't lost its fizz. It's remarkable how something so old and so perishable can have lasted so well.

It's funny how the past can so often catch up with us, sometimes in a nice way, but sometimes in a disagreeable one. Most of us remember something unpleasant from the

---

[9] Martin O'Neill was manager of Leicester City football Club from 1995 to 2000. LCFC won the Football League Cup under O'Neill in 1997 and 2000, as well as losing the final in 1999. They finished ninth in the Premiership in 1997. tenth in 1998 and 1999, and eighth in 2000. The two League Cup triumphs saw them qualify for the UEFA Cup each time. Many LCFC fans yearn for O'Neill's return, for these were the golden years. See my *Thought* "Whelmed" 2 June 2000.

past. Maybe it's something we said or did that keeps pricking our conscience. Perhaps we bear a grudge against someone who did something to us. Perhaps there's something we should have done but haven't. Maybe we're dreading being found out. These things can be a burden.

Now there is something we can do about this. Jesus taught us to pray: *For if you forgive men when they sin against you, your heavenly Father will also forgive you*[10]. We can ask forgiveness only when we forgive the people who have wronged us. That's what Jesus' words mean. You see, God knows that when we forgive others, then, and only then, will we be able to receive forgiveness from other people, and from God Himself. If we can forgive people who have hurt us, then God will forgive us for the things that hurt Him.

The things that hurt God are all the things we do which fall short of His standards. Jesus summed those standards up in the two key commandments: to love God and to love our neighbour as ourself. But we're not so hot on the Commandments these days. How many of us could name all ten? There's a story that a Jewish Rabbi remarked to a Christian minister "You took the Ten Commandments from us". "Certainly," came the reply, "but you can't accuse us of keeping them!"

Well, how about giving them a try, starting today?

---

[10] Matthew 6:13-15 NIVUK

CHILDREN IN NEED

FRIDAY 20 NOVEMBER 1998

Those of us who are parents will understand the joke that says, "Madness is hereditary. You inherit it from your children". Having children causes all sorts of problems. Choosing a name for your child is difficult enough. You have to choose a name that will suit them, whatever their path in life. You have to watch out for initials that spell something unfortunate. And there are names that you just can't choose, like Adolf, I suppose.

And it doesn't stop there. Children are a great responsibility. You have to wash them and change them, feed them and nurse them, clothe them and teach them. The one thing you don't *have* to do as a parent is to love them, because that love comes naturally. It's one of the strongest attachments known to mankind. Parents are willing to sacrifice their own lives to protect their children.

That's why news reports of the abuse and even the murders of young children cause us such anger. It's a denial of everything that children mean to us, our hopes for the future. Only yesterday, there were news reports that a grave had been uncovered in Colombia that contained the bodies of thirteen street children. In that country, it seems, if you're a child who's so poor that you haven't got a roof over your head, then that's enough to make you a murder target for vigilante gangs.

That sort of cruelty is so unnatural that we are appalled and angered by it. But here in Leicester and Leicestershire there are children who have to roam the cold streets after school until a parent comes home and lets them in. There are children who are inadequately fed, who miss out on things like learning to play a musical instrument, or school trips abroad, even proper places to play in safety. It's often not the fault of the parents, who sacrifice their own well-being to provide the basics for their children. But if you're bringing up a family on your own with only state benefits to sustain you, life is one long uphill struggle.

It's Children in Need day today, which aims to provide things for children who genuinely need them. Let's give generously. It's what God wants. Jesus had a special place in his heart for children. *Let the children come to Me,* He said, *Don't stop them! For the Kingdom of Heaven belongs to such as these.*[11]

---

[11] Matthew 19:14 NLT

MOTIVES

Headache? Sneezing? Muzzy-headed? Sweating? Sore throat? Feeling awful? Sounds as if you might've got 'flu. You'd be in good company, though, because there's an epidemic of it. And if you haven't got it, I bet you know someone who *has* got it. Or had it. And unless your doctor thinks otherwise, there's not much you can do but sweat it out. It's not much fun. You're really on your own with 'flu.

Other people can try to make you feel better, though.

There was a mother who was sick in bed with 'flu one day when her darling little daughter decided to play nurse. The little girl fluffed up the pillows in her mummy's bed, brought her a vase of freshly cut flowers from the garden, and even brought her a warm cup of tea. "I didn't know you even knew how to make tea," said the mother. "It's delicious. What a wonderful surprise." "Oh yes, Mummy," said the little girl. "I learned watching you. I boiled the water, put the tea leaves in, and strained it into a cup. I couldn't find a strainer, though, so I used the flyswatter." "You what!" screamed the mother, horrified. "Oh, don't worry, Mummy. I didn't use the *new* flyswatter."

I remember an occasion when my son, then aged four, proudly brought my wife and me breakfast in bed. He brought us tea and boiled eggs. Now, we had not at this point in his young life shown him how to boil a kettle or put a saucepan on to boil. So the tea was made with cold water, and the eggs, duly immersed for three minutes by the egg timer in cold water, were raw. But I can tell you it was one of the most enjoyable and memorable meals of my life. Not because of the food and drink, but because of the love with which it had been prepared.

Just like at Christmas, when we say, "It's the thought that counts" on receiving gifts from our loved ones, the motive behind our actions is more important than what we actually do.

You see, God looks into our hearts and sees our real motives. And He promises a reward in heaven for those who do good things for other people out of love.

So, here's a thought: is there a good deed *you* could do today? - if you've not got the 'flu, of course!

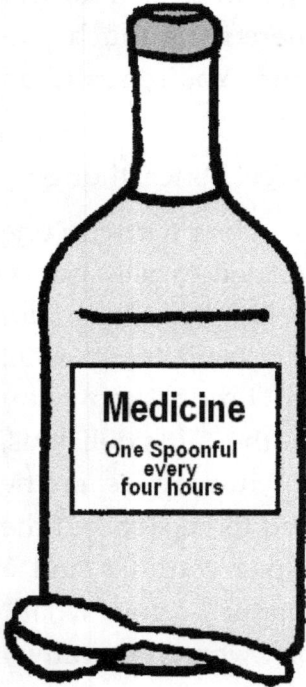

Medicine
One Spoonful
every
four hours

DEATH

WEDNESDAY 10 FEBRUARY 1999

When I'm on holiday, one of the things I like to do is look around old churches. I like finding curious epitaphs on gravestones. Up in the north of England I saw one, which read:

Remember, friend, when passing by
As you are now, so once was I
As I am now, soon you will be
Prepare for death and follow me.

Underneath this worthy Victorian verse someone had scratched another two lines:

To follow you I'm not content
Until I know which way you went

Someone once said that the riskiest activity of all is living – because it has a 100% fatality rate. And we all know the old cliché that there are only two certain things in life: death and taxes.

If your family is like mine, we're so scattered around the country – indeed the world – the only time we ever get together is at a family funeral. At the funeral of King Hussein of Jordan this week, the world family gathered. They say there's never been such a meeting of the truly powerful people of all the major countries of the world. There were princes and presidents and prime ministers, gathered together to pay their respects to someone who had become one of the great peacemakers of modern times. And Jesus said, *Blessed are the peacemakers, for they will be called sons of God[12].* The world's sense of loss brought representatives of nations that had recently been at war, and even some who were engaged in military stand-offs at that very moment. It was a quite remarkable assembly of the great, the good, and the not-so-great-or-good.

By contrast, the great novelist and philosopher Dame Iris Murdoch, who died this week, left instructions that there was to be no ceremony, no service, and no memorial to mark her passing. She wishes to go without formality.

I wonder whether she was right. Because funerals are not for the benefit of the dead, but to help those who are left behind come to terms with their loss. A good funeral reinforces the happy memories we have, and we celebrate the life that has just come to an end. And Jesus said, *Blessed are those who mourn, for they will be comforted[13].*

Christians have a sure belief that when they die, they will rise to heaven. None of that Hoddle reincarnation business[14] for us. When a Christian dies, we know which way he's going. Now, here's a thought: do you know which way *you're* going?

---

[12] Matthew 5:9 NIVUK

[13] Matthew 5:4 NIVUK

[14] Glenn Hoddle, a career footballer and manager, was sacked from his job as head coach of the English football team for saying "You and I have been physically given two hands and two legs and a half-decent brain. Some people have not been born like that for a reason. The karma is working from another lifetime." (Interview with Matt Dickinson of *The Times* newspaper, 30 January 1999) There was widespread condemnation of this from sporting bodies, disablement campaigners and the government. Hoddle apologized and retracted his remarks, but the Football Association terminated his contract on 2 February 1999.

MOTHERS

MONDAY 15 MARCH 1999

Are you old enough to remember the washing powder advert that asked, "What is a Mum?" The answer *they* wanted you to give was "the person who washes my clothes", true enough but I think there's a bit more to being a Mum than that. Mums give birth to you, they bring you up and look after you until you're grown up – and for a long time after that, too. The main thing is, *they love you.*

Yesterday was Mothering Sunday, started for the benefit of young servant-girls in the seventeenth to nineteenth centuries. It was the one Sunday in the year those hard-working girls were guaranteed to have off so they could visit their mothers. And so the custom has come down to us, and we visit our mothers if we can, and write to them or phone them if it's impossible to get to see them, and remember them with love and affection if they are no longer with us.

Everyone has or had a mum – except of course for Adam and Eve, who were made directly by God, who was Father *and* Mother to them, I suppose. Even Jesus, fathered by the Holy Spirit, had a mother – the young girl Mary. Mary loved and cared for Jesus from before His birth, right through to the end of His life. She even stood by the cross as he was cruelly executed. And Jesus loved and looked after

Mary, remembering to give her into the care of His closest friend just before He breathed His last[15].

Remembering things can be difficult. An elderly couple were concerned they were starting to forget things, so they went to see their doctor. He confirmed that they were in good physical shape, but told them that it wasn't unusual to become forgetful as they got older. He suggested that they start writing things down. That night the husband went to the kitchen to make a cup of tea and asked his wife if she wanted anything. "Some ice-cream" she said, "write it down". "No, I'll remember," said the husband. "And some strawberries. Write it down." "No, I'll remember." "And some whipped cream. Write it down." "No, I'll remember". He went to the kitchen, came back twenty minutes later with a plate of fried eggs, bacon, sausages, and baked beans. The wife stared at it for a moment and said, "Where's my toast?"

One of the Ten Commandments, repeated by Jesus, is *Honour your Father and Mother*[16].

<u>He</u> did. Do <u>you</u>?

ה. כַּבֵּד אֶת־אָבִיךָ וְאֶת־אִמֶּךָ

ve-'et-i-me-kha	'et-'a-vi-kha	kab-bed
and your mother	*your father*	*Honor !*

---

[15] *While the soldiers were looking after themselves, Jesus' mother, his aunt, Mary the wife of Clopas, and Mary Magdalene stood at the foot of the cross. Jesus saw his mother and the disciple he loved standing near her. He said to his mother, "Woman, here is your son." Then to the disciple, "Here is your mother." From that moment the disciple accepted her as his own mother.*
John 19:24-27 MSG
[16] Matthew 19:19 NIVUK and MSG and NLT – and doubtless any other translation you can lay your hands on.

14

DECLINING STANDARDS[17]

WEDNESDAY 5 MAY 1999

Yesterday, the little Baptist chapel at Stocking Farm was vandalised. Bibles were torn up, glass and furniture was smashed. The church is too poor to be able to put things right. So the people who have been worshipping there for the last 44 years will have nowhere to meet, all because someone's idea of fun is to spoil things for other people.

A different attack on the church came yesterday from, of all people, the Broadcasting Standards Commission. Their report said it is offensive to non-Christians for broadcasters to use the expressions "AD" and "BC". Instead we are supposed to say "CE" (that's "Christian Era") instead of AD or Anno Domini, and "BCE" (that's Before the Christian Era) for BC or "before Christ"[18]. Well, let me tell the Commission that *I'm* offended by their patronising attempt to throw away two thousand years of our cultural heritage in their pursuit of political correctness.

---

[17] I had dozens of letters and phone calls from listeners agreeing with my sentiments in this talk.

[18] Professor David Craig of Middlesex University was commissioned by the BSC to prepare a study, in which he wrote, "The inconvenience of using CE and BCE instead of the more traditional and less sensitive BC and AD is modest compared with the offence occasioned by the *Anno Domini* and Before Christ dating. The assumption that Christianity has the sole claim to virtue and value is offensive to all religions. The sensitivities of Muslims, Jews, Buddhists, Hindus and Sikhs have to be taken into account in modern Britain." To be fair, the BSC was less than lukewarm in its acceptance of the study.

But perhaps this is symptomatic of society as a whole. Here're some trivialities that tell me that standards of behaviour are slipping:

- ❖ Look on the pavements of our towns and cities (not to mention your shoes): there's chewing gum casually discarded.

- ❖ Look at the walls of any unguarded building in our towns and cities and you'll see tasteless graffiti sprayed all over them.

- ❖ Look outside any fast food outlet in our towns and cities and you'll see plastic and paper wrappers thrown onto the floor, often with an empty litter bin a couple of steps away.

- ❖ Hold a shop door open for the person following you and you hardly ever get thanked.

- ❖ When was the last time you saw someone giving up a seat on the bus for someone who really needs to sit down?

- ❖ I'm deeply offended by the casual use of God's name as an exclamation. Have you noticed; in that TV programme "Changing Rooms"[19], when the refurbished room is revealed to the owner, they almost invariably shriek "Oh my God!"

---

[19] A home improvement show broadcast in the United Kingdom on BBC Television from 1996 to 2004. The concept of the show was for couples to swap houses with friends or neighbours with each pair decorating and furnishing a room in each other's homes to a barely adequate budget. They had the advice of some famous "designers", whose ambitious ideas were sometimes a shock to the householders when the "improvement" was revealed.

I guess this is all part of the tendency for human beings to sink to the lowest common denominator. At its worst, we see it in the people who set off nail bombs and the depths to which the Serbian militia has sunk in the atrocities repeatedly reported from Kosovo[20].

Truly, "There is no health in us[21]".

But Jesus offers us a way out. He said, *Love God, and love your neighbour*[22]. With more care for our neighbour, and more consideration for our neighbour and, yes, more love for our neighbour, the world *would* be a better place.

And that starts with you and me.

---

[20] Nine Serbian and Yugoslavian leaders and senior militia (including Slobodan Milošević) had just had allegations lodged against them that they directed, encouraged or supported a campaign of terror and violence directed at Kosovo Albanian civilians, with a view to ethnically cleanse the territory they had taken. Much later, in 2006, they were accused of murdering 919 named men, women, children and babies.

[21] *Almightie and most merciful father, we have erred and straied from thy waies, lyke lost sheepe we have folowed to much the devises and desires of our owne hartes. We have offended against thy holy lawes: We have left undone those thinges whiche we ought to have done, and we have done those thinges which we ought not to have done, and <u>there is no health in us</u>, but thou, O Lorde, have mercy upon us miserable offerdours. Spare thou them O God, whiche confesse their faultes. Restore thou them that be penitent, accordyng to thy promises declared unto mankynde, in Christe Jesu our Lorde. And graunt, O most merciful father, for his sake, that we may hereafter lyve a godly, ryghtuous, and sobre life, to the glory of thy holy name. Amen.*
General Confession, Book of Common Prayer, 1559

[22] In full: Love the Lord your God with all your heart and with all your soul and with all your mind. This is the first and greatest commandment. And the second is like it: Love your neighbour as yourself.
Matthew 22:37-39 NIVUK

STUFF HAPPENS

WEDNESDAY 26 MAY 1999

Two vampire bats were hanging upside down. One of them – let's call him Stewart, since he was the opening bat - said, "I'm hungry" and flew off. Two hours later, he returned and hung himself upside down again. "How did you get on, Stewart?" asked the other. "Terrible. Not a living creature out there. Not a drop of blood to be seen. I'm famished." "So am I," said Hussein (for he was second bat). "*I'll* go to look for some nice fresh blood." He flew off and two minutes later he came back in and hung himself upside down. Stewart looked at him. Hussein was simply soaked with blood. It was all over his fur and was dripping off him. "Hey, Hussein, old vampire bat chum," said Stewart, "where did you get *that*?" "Well, you see that old oak tree over there?" replied Hussein. "Ye-e-e-s." "Well *I* didn't!"[23]

Isn't life strange that way? You can be engrossed, doing what you're doing, when suddenly, wallop! from nowhere, something you weren't expecting can come up and throw all your plans awry. Last Saturday evening, Lawrence Dallaglio[24] was expecting to fly out today to captain his

---

[23] At this time, Alec Stewart OBE was the opening bat and wicketkeeper for the English cricket team, and Nasser Hussein OBE batted at number two. They were both at the height of their prowess.

[24] Lawrence Dallaglio OBE, up to the previous weekend, was the English Rugby Union captain. The *News of the World,* the Sunday previous to this broadcast, had printed an interview with him in which he bragged of using and dealing in hard drugs, including cocaine and ecstasy. He was also reported as boasting about taking drugs at a party during the Lions

country's rugby team in the World Cup. Thirty-six hours later, he had been forced to resign and spend the next few weeks stuck at home. Last week, Benyamin Netanyahu was Prime Minister of Israel. Today, thrown out of office by the election, he's just an ex-politician looking for a job[25].

All of us suffer disappointments in life. Maybe you don't get the job you really want. Maybe you miss out on a promotion. Maybe a customer or a supplier lets you down. Maybe your love for someone is thrown back at you. Maybe your loved one dies. Maybe ….. oh, so many maybes!

Jesus knew a thing or two about life not working out as you'd hoped. Jesus came to preach good news to the spiritually poor; but He was vilified by the religious leaders of His day. Jesus taught and lived with twelve special friends, but one took money to betray Him to the Secret Police. The friend that Jesus commissioned to do some of the most important work in the church denied at one point that he had known Jesus. The crowd that had cheered Jesus into Jerusalem turned, within a few days, into a mob demanding His execution. But Jesus didn't give up: He went right on to the end. And this is how Jesus encouraged the apostle Paul, who had plenty of set-backs himself: *My grace is sufficient for thee, for My strength is made perfect in weakness[26]*.

Jesus' words encourage me. Do they encourage you?

---

tour to South Africa, in 1997. The RFU quickly replaced him as captain with Martin Johnson CBE. Dallaglio later denied what he had claimed, but it was too late.

[25] Not for long. He returned as Israel's foreign minister in 2002, then various ministerial appointments, while fighting sundry members of the fractious Likud Party. He became Prime Minister again in 2009.

[26] 2 Corinthians 12:9 KJV21C

GUILT

WEDNESDAY 30 JUNE 1999

The July fortnight is just around the corner. Are you going on holiday? Excited? Is it Skeggie or Torremolinos? At least you don't need a passport for Skeggie. But if you're jetting off abroad at the weekend, I hope your passport's ready. 'Cause if it isn't, you might not be going after all! They say there's a million passport applications queuing up to be processed. Apparently, according to a government minister, it's not the Passport Office's inefficiency or the Government forcing even new-born babies to have their own passport that's the cause of the problem. Oh no. The problem is *you*. If no one had applied for a passport, there wouldn't be any backlog! Simple as leaves on the line, or the wrong sort of snow.[27]

Everyone tries to pass the buck, don't they? It started in the Garden of Eden. God asked Adam "Why did you eat the forbidden fruit?" And Adam said "It wasn't my fault. It was Eve that made me do it." And Eve said "It wasn't my

---

[27] Mike O'Brien, Secretary of State for the Home Department: "Passport applications are taking longer than normal to process at the Liverpool office as a result of operational problems arising from the implementation of new high technology driven passport issuing arrangements. Also, Liverpool are dealing with very high seasonal demand for passports with intake of applications since April 1999 over 20 per cent. up on the same period in 1998". (Hansard, 26 May 1999)

fault either. It was the snake that told me to do it." And the snake … didn't have a leg to stand on!

Be that as it may … sometimes there's no one we can pass the buck to. We know, deep down inside, it was our fault. If we hadn't done that, then … If we hadn't said that, then … If we hadn't been there, then … Christians call that pricking of our conscience by a special word. That word is "guilt". And guilt is a nasty thing. It gnaws away at us and makes us feel blameworthy. It gives us feelings of inadequacy and makes us feel we're less than God made us to be. And there's only one way for us to deal with guilt, and that's to ask for forgiveness for the sin we committed in the first place.

We can ask the person we've wronged to forgive us. And maybe they will, maybe they won't. But sometimes we don't know who to ask forgiveness from. Sometimes we don't know how to ask them for forgiveness. Sometimes we can't ask for forgiveness because it was a long time ago and the person has since died.

That's when we can turn to Jesus to forgive us, to take away our sin. All we have to do is ask. And Jesus lets us pass the buck to him. It's as if He gives us a fresh, crisp, passport with an open visa to heaven. And there's no backlog problem there.

WORDS MATTER

Some of you might know that on alternate weeks I do a review of the Sunday papers on BBC Radio Leicester's *Morning Extra* programme on Sunday mornings. Yesterday's papers were proof that we're in the "silly season", when there's not much hard news about. So there were no major stories that were covered in every paper, no scoops to make us all say "wow", nothing to change governments. The few journalists who are not on holiday themselves, flounder around, printing stories that have been gathering dust for months, and even making up stories about nothing. Gossip becomes news. Trivia is magnified. So at this time of year we can expect to read of crop circles; and cabinet reshuffles that don't happen; of Archbishops who are believed to possibly be going to reject some central article of faith in some speech they haven't yet drafted; of football transfers that never in fact happen.

But here are some genuine newspaper headlines that I've cherished over the years:

- **RED TAPE HOLDS UP NEW BRIDGES**
- **CHILDREN MAKE NUTRITIOUS SNACKS**
- **ENRAGED COW INJURES FARMER WITH AXE**
- **STOLEN PAINTING FOUND BY TREE**

And my personal favourite,

- **CRASHED PLANE FLEW TOO CLOSE TO GROUND, EXPERT SAYS**

It's very easy to express yourself badly, and that can lead to misunderstandings. I wonder if, like me, you sometimes find yourself ignoring the old saying "Put brain into gear before engaging mouth". I once found myself asking whether someone's father was up and about again when I had attended his funeral just a couple of weeks earlier. And boy, did I cringe when I realised! It taught me that you really do have to be careful about what you say.

Jesus had a half-brother called James. Around 50 AD, he wrote a letter to Jewish converts to Christianity. He warns *them* to be careful to control what they say[28]. He says our tongue is like the rudder of a ship. It is small, but it has disproportionate effects. He remarks that just as a forest fire can start with just a tiny spark, likewise the words we speak can have unforeseeable effects.

So my thought for us today is to think twice before we say something unpleasant about someone else; to hold back before we pass on a delicious piece of gossip or tittle-tattle. In short, to watch our tongue.

Let's make today a sensible day in the middle of a silly season.

---

[28] In full: *Take ships as an example. Although they are so large and are driven by strong winds, they are steered by a very small rudder wherever the pilot wants to go. Likewise the tongue is a small part of the body, but it makes great boasts. Consider what a great forest is set on fire by a small spark. The tongue also is a fire, a world of evil among the parts of the body. It corrupts the whole person, sets the whole course of his life on fire, and is itself set on fire by hell. All kinds of animals, birds, reptiles and creatures of the sea are being tamed and have been tamed by man, but no man can tame the tongue.* (James 3:4-8 NIVUK)

NAMES

WEDNESDAY 15 SEPTEMBER 1999

Well, Patsy and Liam Gallagher have done it. Had a baby, that is. "Who?" you ask. Come on! This is Cool Britannia[29], man. *Liam*. You know, the geezer from Oasis. What? Oasis is a celebrated beat combo, me lud. And Patsy? She's his wife – and a MAW. What? A MAW – M. A. W. – Model, Actress, Whatever. Anyway, they're very famous. And Patsy has just become a Ma as well as a MAW. And they've called their baby son "Lennon" in tribute to John Lennon. I bet the poor kid ends up being called Len!

Pop music people have a habit of giving bizarre names to their offspring. What about these: Zowie Bowie (poor old Zowie changed his name to Joe Jones when he was older, and can you blame him?); Fifi Trixibelle Geldof and her half-sister Heavenly Hiraani Tiger Lily; Dweezil and Moon Unit Zappa. Actually, I think the winner in the "loony names for the kids of famous parents" stakes must be Bono from U2. Last week he named his son Elijah Bob Patricius Guggi Q Hewson. It's true, I tell you!

Perhaps we're all getting more adventurous in naming children. The recent Oxford Dictionary of names includes some new ones on me, like: Ace, Baron, Beige, Bijou, Gobnat, Gypsy, Jazz, Raven, Stone, and Zenith.

---

[29] A catchphrase used heavily by the "New Labour" government under relatively young Prime Minister Tony Blair from 1997. It was originally the title of a 1967 song by the Bonzo Dog Doodah Band, and later as the name of a variety of Ben and Jerry's ice-cream (Vanilla & Strawberries and chocolate shortbread).

Naming a baby is a serious business. You sort of mark the child for life. Apologies if there are any real life examples out there, but you can't imagine a Marmaduke tarmacing your driveway, can you? And what about His Royal Highness King Gobnat? It doesn't ring true, does it?

Four out of the top five boys' names today are straight from the Bible: Thomas, James, Daniel and Joshua[30]. It's difficult to go wrong with the standard biblical names.

Well, actually it is. You don't want to call your child Maher-shalal-hashbaz[31] or Zerubbabel[32] for instance! But all biblical names have a meaning.

Thomas means "a twin" (don't ask me what you're supposed to call the other one!); James means "the substitute"; Daniel means "God is my judge"; and Joshua... well, that's the same as "Jesus" and it means "the one who saves and heals and restores". Because Jesus came into the world to save sinners like me and you, and heal our hurts, and restore us to God's favour.

And that's why Christians say that Jesus is the Name above all other names.

---

[30] The other was Jack, which can be a derivative of John or Jacob, both biblical names themselves. The top five girls' names were Chloe, Emily, Megan, Olivia and Sophie, none of them biblical.

[31] Apparently it means something like "Hurrying to the spoil, he has made haste to the plunder".

[32] Zerubbabel means something like "the one sown of Babylon", referring to a child conceived and born in Babylon. Check out the modern celebrity parallel: David Beckham's son, Brooklyn.

COMPASSION

WEDNESDAY 6 OCTOBER 1999

Yesterday morning, a few hundred people were on their way to work. It was an ordinary day. Last weekend was gone and forgotten, and next weekend too far away to think about. And suddenly, their world was changed forever, as their train collided with another just outside Paddington Station in London[33]. In just a few seconds, some had lost their lives, some had been seriously injured, and others were bruised and battered and shocked.

And that is a bleak and terrible story. But there were good things too. The fire brigade was quickly on the scene and acted in the highest traditions of their service. They saved many lives as they extricated the injured from the wreckage. The paramedic services were also in attendance, rendering aid to the injured. And the hospitals brought their

---

[33] The disaster occurred at 08:09 BST on 5 October 1999, when a Thames Trains three-car train collided with a First Great Western High Speed Train of eight passenger carriages at Ladbroke Grove Junction, about two miles west of the terminus at London Paddington station. The trains collided almost head-on at the junction with a combined closing speed of approximately 130 mph.

The first car of the Thames train, the 0806 from Paddington to Bedwyn, Wiltshire, was totally destroyed on impact, and the diesel fuel carried by this train at the start of its daily journey ignited, causing a series of separate fires in the wreckage, particularly in coach H at the front of the HST, which was completely burnt out. Thirty one people, including the drivers of both trains, were killed, and 227 people were admitted to hospital. A further 296 people were treated at the site of the crash for minor injuries.

emergency procedures into action, with teams of surgeons and nurses and others working hard to save lives and restore broken bodies.

And the ordinary people of Paddington lent a hand too. Some were early on the scene and helped dazed survivors to safety. Others came out of their houses with blankets. And the local supermarket made its coffee shop a haven for those with minor injuries, and furnished them and rescue workers with tea and coffee.

And these ordinary people, the firemen and ambulance men and paramedics and railway officials and passengers and the man and woman in the street, are in truth remarkable in their selflessness and care and concern for those afflicted by the disaster.

It is a basic human instinct to rally round the distressed. Time and time again, we have seen an extraordinary response to the needs of our fellow men and women. The international teams who swung into action in the recent earthquakes in Turkey and Taiwan, the people who organised and went with relief supplies for the devastated people of Kosovo, and the generous response to famine victims in Ethiopia and elsewhere have all gladdened our hearts in recent years.

And I dare to suggest that this compassion is something planted deep within us by our Creator-God. For in the beginning, when God created man, He created men and women in His own image. And God is love; and His love is given to us all to share and use and demonstrate. And yesterday He used those firemen and medics and all the others, to show to a cynical world the power of love.

BACK IN TOUCH

MONDAY 6 DECEMBER 1999

Life is full of little irritations, isn't it? You know:

♦ You programme the video recorder for the wrong channel and get some awful American chat show instead of that film you wanted.
♦ Or you leave a paper hanky in your pocket when you put it in the washing machine and everything comes out covered in white fluff.
♦ Or you've bought a Christmas present for someone and you get it out of the box to check it's not broken before you wrap it, and the wretched thing just *won't* go back in the way it came.
♦ Or what happened to me when I was preparing this Thought for the Day: you reach under the table to pick something off the floor and smash your head on the way up.

Some calamities are a bit bigger, though. Those NASA scientists must be pretty cheesed off that their £135 million Mars Lander seems to have got the hump and won't speak to them. It seems they've lost touch and have pretty much given up hope of getting anything out of the exercise – at least that was the case up to the moment I banged my head.[34]

---

[34] The Mars Climate Orbiter was one of two NASA spacecraft in the Mars Surveyor '98 program, the other being the Mars Polar Lander. The two missions were to study the Martian weather, climate, water and carbon dioxide, among other things. It was intended to enter orbit at an altitude of 140–150 km above Mars. However, a navigation error caused the

Losing touch is something that happens. I can still remember the boys' class register when I was in class 2/1 at Mayflower Junior School in the 1950s: Banks, Bates, Burgin, Day, Denney..... And out of the eighteen boys in the class, I've hardly been in touch with any of them since our schooldays. I *did* hear that one had become a multi-millionaire on the Lottery, though; another is in prison and at least one is dead.

We can, of course, lose touch with close family members, too. Sons and daughters, brothers and sisters go their separate ways, moving to other parts of this global village we inhabit. And sometimes rifts can develop and we just don't meet with relatives who live within a mile or two.

The four weeks leading to Christmas is called the Advent season by the Church. *This* Christmas we're celebrating the fact that two thousand years ago God reconnected with the human race. We had drifted apart. So He got back in touch by sending Jesus, His Son, to meet with you and me, the people He loves.

Maybe this advent season is a time for *us* to get back in touch, not just with lost friends and relatives – but with God Himself.

---

spacecraft to reach as low as 57 km. The spacecraft was destroyed by atmospheric stresses and friction at this low altitude. The navigation error arose because NASA subcontractor Lockheed Martin used Imperial units instead of the metric system used in all other calculations by NASA.

JUSTICE

MONDAY 17 JANUARY 2000

I see that Mike Tyson finally arrived yesterday by Concorde to prepare for a boxing match in a couple of week's time. It was only by the Home Secretary intervening that he was allowed to enter the country. Apparently, a convicted foreign national who has served more than 12 months in prison can only be allowed into Britain if "exceptional compassionate circumstances" apply. And Jack Straw has decided to be "compassionate". Not actually to Mike Tyson, but to all the small businesses that stand to lose money if the fight does not take place. For Mike Tyson was convicted of the rape of an eighteen year old girl in 1991 and went to prison[35]. Various pressure groups are campaigning to have Mr Straw's decision reversed, and Tyson sent home.

And I also see that Myra Hindley, one of the Moors Murderers[36], has been receiving treatment for a potentially fatal brain condition in Addenbrooke's Hospital in Cambridge. The hospital's administrative director said there had been a "number of representations" from the public who objected to the child killer receiving treatment.

---

[35] He was sentenced to six years' imprisonment and served three.

[36] Ian Brady and Myra Hindley, his lover, were convicted of the sadistic murders of three children, and later confessed to two more. Hindley eventually died in November 2002; while at the time of compilation of this book, Brady remains alive (though taking inadequate nourishment, apparently) and resident in a secure mental hospital facility.

Although both of these cases have many strands, I wonder if there is a common thread that runs through them both. Mike Tyson and Myra Hindley were convicted of contemptible crimes. No one can condone their terrible deeds. Their prison sentences are richly deserved. But the reaction of pressure groups and individuals to Mike Tyson's arrival, and the claims of some that Myra Hindley should not receive medical treatment, both seek to heap further punishment on top of the sentences already meted out. Vindictiveness is at work here, and there is no place for that in a just, civilised, democratic and – yes! – Christian country like ours.

Seventeen days ago, the world celebrated two thousand years of Christianity, and one of the overwhelming themes in Christ's teaching is Justice. But Justice tempered with Mercy. For one of the other great themes of Christianity is forgiveness. The prayer that Jesus taught says *forgive us our trespasses, as we forgive those who trespass against us*[37].

Now, we are not the ones "trespassed against" by Tyson or Hindley, so we are not directly in a position to forgive them. But we can see that both justice and mercy are exercised in their cases.

Jesus said, *Do not judge, or you too will be judged. For in the same way as you judge others, you will be judged, and with the measure you use, it will be measured to you.*[38]

---

[37] This is from the 1662 Book of Common Prayer version of Matthew 6:12. The most common translation from the KJV onwards is for *debts* rather than *trespasses*, but the usage has stuck.
[38] Matthew 7:1-2 NIVUK

WHATSOEVER A MAN SOWETH ...[39]

FRIDAY 18 FEBRUARY 2000

It was quite chilly yesterday at Filbert Street. It wasn't the overnight frost that caused it. No, it was Martin O'Neill laying into Stan Collymore and the rest of the team for their tomfoolery in the bar of the sports club in Spain[40]. Grown men should have known better than to let their high spirits get the better of them. And Martin O'Neill didn't mess about: he imposed severe penalties on the guilty men and made them pay personally for the costs involved.

Teresa Gorman MP was carpeted yesterday too. A House of Commons committee found she had failed to register her financial interests in the register of members' interests. She had even taken part in the debates on the subject of landlords and tenants when in effect, secretly, she is one. The committee hasn't messed around either: they've recommended she be excluded from the House of Commons for a whole month.

And over in Germany, more and more revelations are coming out about the corrupt funding of the Christian Democrat Party[41] under former Chancellor Kohl. The party and several senior politicians are being exposed as dishonest and devious. Maybe even criminal fraud is involved. This

---

[39] *Be not deceived, God is not mocked; for whatsoever a man soweth, that shall he also reap.* Galatians 6:7 KJV21C

[40] Leicester City FC cut short a mid-season break at the luxurious sporting resort of La Manga in Spain after newly-signed Stan Collymore alarmed other guests by letting off a fire extinguisher in a bar.

[41] *Christlich Demokratische Union Deutschlands.* Not very "Christian" if truth be known, and some say not quite "democratic", either.

story is going to run and run, but already several political heads have rolled, and it looks as if things are going to get worse for the Christian Democrats, who are coming out as rather undemocratic and certainly far removed from Christian standards of behaviour.

Quite a lot of chickens have come home to roost this week, at Filbert Street, at Westminster, and in Berlin.

One day, Christians believe we shall *all* have to account for our actions. We call it the Day of Judgement. God will judge everyone. Everything bad we've thought, everything bad we've said, everything bad we've done, everything good we should have done but didn't, will be recited before Him, and He will judge us accordingly. Christians, though, will find that all the wrong things in their lives have been erased from the record, because Jesus has forgiven their sins.

And back here, we've still got a chance to do something about our attitudes and lifestyle. We can ask Jesus for forgiveness; in the words of the Lord's Prayer: *forgive us our trespasses*[42]. And in these times of 10 pence rise on the minimum wage[43] and 75 pence rises on the state pension, it's sobering to remember that the wages of sin are exactly the same as they always were[44].

---

[42] See the previous *Thought*.

[43] The national adult minimum wage from 1 April 1999 was £3.60 per hour. From 1 October 2000, it was to become £3.70.

[44] *For the wages of sin is death, but the gift of God is eternal life in Christ Jesus our Lord.* Romans 6:23 NIVUK

PAYING OUR FAIR WHACK

WEDNESDAY 22 MARCH 2000

So. No more secrets. The Chancellor has spoken. The budget has been announced. And depending on our circumstances and whether we smoke or drink or drive, we might be a little better off, or a little worse off.

As they say, there's only two things in life that are certain: death and taxes. Although income tax has only been around for a couple of centuries, before that there were all sorts of taxes that people had to pay.

There used to be a window tax[45] that led to people living in dark and gloomy rooms because they couldn't afford to pay up.

There was a poll tax in the 14th Century[46] that led to the peasants' revolt led by Wat Tyler and Jack Straw. No, not *him!*[47]

Even the famous Domesday Book was compiled so that William the Conqueror could tax the kingdom he had acquired.

One of England's great historical figures, John Wyclif[48], who was Rector of Lutterworth in the 1380s, preached against the taxes demanded by the Pope. Every

---

[45] A section of the *Act of Making Good the Deficiency of the Clipped Money, 1696,* repealed finally in 1851.

[46] Introduced by John of Gaunt and levied three times, in 1377 (1 groat [fourpence] for everyone over 14 yrs)

[47] Jack Straw was at the time of the broadcast Home Secretary.

[48] Variously Wycliffe, Wycliff, Wiclef, Wicliffe, or Wickliffe

hearth[49] had to pay a penny – and that's when a penny would feed a family for a week and still have something left over. Those "Peter's Pence" (as they were called) were sent to support the corrupt Roman churchmen, who lived in luxury at the expense of the poor and needy.

Jesus taught us something about paying our taxes. In His time, the Romans had conquered Israel and demanded heavy taxes from the Israelites. There was a spirit of rebellion against paying the tax, and someone asked Jesus whether it was right to pay.

This was a trick question. If Jesus said, "don't pay", Roman spies would have him arrested for stirring up rebellion. If Jesus said, "Pay the tax", then Jesus would be branded a collaborator with the enemy and therefore an enemy of God and the Jews.

A denarius of Tiberius Caesar
r. 14-37AD

But Jesus was cleverer than them. He borrowed a coin, and, showing the head of Caesar on one side of the coin said, "Give to Caesar what belongs to Caesar".

---

[49] i.e. every home: the hearth was where the fire was kept, to warm the dwelling and cook the food. Home is where the hearth is.

A denarius of the time of Jesus

And then he flipped the coin over and showed the other side, where there was a picture of an olive branch, which the Jews knew as a symbol of God's love for them. And Jesus went on: "And give to God what belongs to God."[50]

And what Jesus is telling *us* is to pay our fair whack. No buying under-the-counter cigarettes or off-the-back-of-a-lorry booze[51]. Because that way, we're stealing from everyone else.

And one of God's rules for a healthy community is: *You shall not steal*[52].

---

[50] This is the full story from Luke 20:20-26 in the NIVUK translation:
Keeping a close watch on him, they sent spies, who pretended to be honest. They hoped to catch Jesus in something he said so that they might hand him over to the power and authority of the governor. So the spies questioned him: Teacher, we know that you speak and teach what is right, and that you do not show partiality but teach the way of God in accordance with the truth. Is it right for us to pay taxes to Caesar or not?
He saw through their duplicity and said to them, *Show me a denarius.* [A Roman coin] *Whose portrait and inscription are on it?* Caesar's, they replied. He said to them, *Then give to Caesar what is Caesar's, and to God what is God's.* They were unable to trap him in what he had said there in public. And astonished by his answer, they became silent.
[51] There had been a spate of finds of vast quantities of smuggled alcohol and tobacco in Leicestershire recently.
[52] Deuteronomy 5:19 NIVUK (one of the "Ten Commandments")

HOT CROSS BUNS

FRIDAY 21 APRIL 2000 – GOOD FRIDAY

B ack in the dawn of history, when I was but a lad in short trousers, grey flannel shirt and chapped knees, I remember a playground chant we used to use:

One a penny, two a penny, Hot cross Buns;
One a penny, two a penny, Hot cross Buns;
Give them to your daughters, give them to your sons,
One a penny, two a penny, Hot cross Buns.

Do children still chant that these days, I wonder, when they're bouncing a pair of tennis balls against a wall, or skipping? Perhaps it would need updating a bit, what with prices being the way they are. 25p a bun seems to be the going rate these days. That's five shillings, as used to was!

And of course, Hot Cross Buns were reserved exclusively for Easter. You couldn't find one in the shops before Good Friday. But *my* local supermarket has been selling them since January[53], alongside Easter eggs, some of which hit the shops immediately after Christmas. If I ruled the world, I'd make a law reserving the sale of everything to its due season[54]. No fireworks until a week before bonfire night, no Christmas goodies until the beginning of December, no Easter eggs until a fortnight before Easter Sunday, no Hot Cross buns 'til Good Friday itself.

I guess we all live in a "wish and get" culture nowadays. If we want something, we want it *now*. Buy now

---

[53] And in 2011, they're available all year round. Shame!
[54] Several listeners took the trouble to phone in to agree with me on this.

and pay later. We can't be bothered to wait. We live life in a rush. We demand instant communication, through our mobile phones and our e-mails. And these things are wonderful, but we let them run our lives a bit too much.

Today, Good Friday, is the most solemn day in the Christian year. It's the day when Christians remember the cruel execution of Jesus outside the walls of Jerusalem around AD 33. Christians, though, call this day "Good" Friday. How can the "judicial" murder of Jesus, God in human form, be considered "Good"?

Because the death of Jesus, in ways no one fully understands, is the price that Jesus paid for our forgiveness. This wasn't a cheap "buy now pay later" transaction. It was a "Come on in to the Kingdom of God; I've paid for you" transaction. It was the greatest deal ever struck.

> *There was no other good enough*
> *To pay the price of sin;*
> *He only could unlock the gate*
> *Of heaven, and let us in.*[55]

I'm off to eat a Hot Cross Bun for breakfast now, and I'll be looking at the cross marked on it, and remembering…

---

[55] Verse 5 from "There is a green hill far away" by Mrs. Cecil Frances Alexander, in *Hymns for Little Children*, 1848

WHELMED

FRIDAY 2 JUNE 2000

People are always on the move these days. A day or two ago, some bloke took off from Spitzbergen in a hot air balloon fitted with a wicker basket, aiming for the North Pole. He eventually landed 12.9 miles away from it. One of his support crew was ecstatic. "He didn't land 50 miles away," crowed the man at base camp. "He didn't land 25 miles away. He couldn't have *got* any closer." Well ... er ... actually, he *could* have got 12.9 miles closer! Perhaps you can tell I'm distinctly underwhelmed with Mr Hempleman-Adams' effort. Incidentally, we've all been overwhelmed by something, but have you ever been just *whelmed*?

But I guess like many of us *I'm* rather whelmed by the news that Martin O'Neill is on the move. He has left Leicester City Football Club and moved oop North. Not as far as 12.9 miles from the North Pole, but certainly to foreign parts to join Celtic Football Club in Glasgow. I'm sure that we wish him well in his new club, despite our disappointment that he has gone. He's given us four and a half years of success and left us in good shape for the European and Premiership challenges for next season. And we hope that the Filbert Street Board will soon come up with a top-flight manager to step into Martin O'Neill's shoes. But I imagine the whole of the City and County is going to be a little unsettled until then.

Changes can be upsetting. There's a truism that the only constant thing in life these days is constant change. Supermarkets are forever switching their displays about confusingly. Road markings get changed overnight. Television programmes start later than advertised because some sporting event overruns, and you come back to find you've videoed the wrong thing[56]. The ways we work are forever changing, and computer systems and the Internet and mobile phones and new bus timetables all add to the pressures of life. And right now, some of you are in a rush to get ready to go out and be off to work, or off to the shops, or off to the doctor's. And in a moment, I've got to be off. People to see, places to go, you know.

But here's an antidote to all the fuss and bother in our daily life.

Jesus said *Peace I leave with you; my peace I give you. I do not give to you as the world gives. Do not let your hearts be troubled and do not be afraid.*[57]

---

[56] This was before the days of Tivo, Sky+ and other more sophisticated recording devices.
[57] John 14:27 NIVUK

DNA

WEDNESDAY 28 JUNE 2000

Monday 26th June 2000 was one of the great days in human achievement. It was described as a "hinge of history". It was the day when the first draft of the human genome was published. The DNA that we have in almost every cell in our body is made up of a coiled up ladder with three billion rungs. And each rung is made up of just four basic chemicals known as A, T, C and G[58]. And because scientists have worked out the long list of rungs on the DNA ladder, great things are being predicted.

They're talking about the cure for all sorts of diseases and conditions like cancer and diabetes and Down's syndrome and many more. They're talking about being able to grow spare parts for your body when they've worn out or been damaged.

But can I chuck a little cold water on the hype surrounding this great achievement? Once they've finalised the map, where are we going, and how long is it going to take? William Harvey demonstrated how the heart worked in 1628, but it wasn't until 1963, 335 years later, that the first heart transplant took place. So it may be a long time before we start to feel any widespread benefits from genome research.

And given that human nature is what it is, how long will it be before some parents start asking for gene therapy to turn their children into beautiful, athletic geniuses?

---

[58] Adenosine, Thymine, Cytosine, Guanine.

41

Although we might yearn for a bit of genetic manipulation so that England can produce a sportsman who can actually *win* something, there is a real worry that unscrupulous people will misuse this information. We desperately need a code of ethics to control what we do with this new knowledge.

But the biggest objection is this: the scientists haven't mapped *me*. They might know which sequence of genes produces my eye colour, which my height, which my balding pate. But even with three billion genes to call on, they don't begin to describe the real me, or the real you. Christians understand that we have a soul, and it can't be broken down into a code. Because that soul, which defines our individuality, our personality, the characteristics that are unique to each one of us, that soul is breathed into us by God.

King David had a real insight in one of his Psalms: *O Lord... you created my inmost being; you knit me together in my mother's womb. I praise You because I am fearfully and wonderfully made.*[59]

So, it's goodbye from me, John Denney, or perhaps you'll know me better as **{FX FADES OUT}** ATCG TAGC CTGA GTAC CATG GACT TACG .....

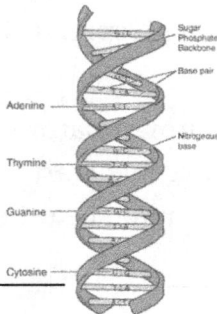

---

[59] Psalm 139:13-14 NIVUK

CONTRADICTIONS IN TERMS
WEDNESDAY 2 AUGUST 2000

This week, scientists have come up with a way of processing eggs that kills off any salmonella bugs. According to the press reports, their secret method uses "natural heat". And that left me wondering. What on earth can *un*natural heat be? It's like all those other odd contradictions in terms you hear from time to time. There's a bar in Granby Street that advertises "Happy *hour*, 5 'til 7". If olive oil is made from olives, what is baby oil made from? A colleague told me his flight to Los Angeles was advertised as "non-stop", but it didn't seem to worry him. And have you ever thought that what we call the *First* Century B.C. is in fact the *last* Century B.C.? The label of a jar of sandwich spread I bought the other day said it was the "New, Improved, Original recipe"! Confused? You bet!

Things can get even more confusing when you go abroad. In a small German hotel I stayed in some years ago, there was a sign on the back of the door of my room. It said: "In case of fire, do your utmost to alarm the hotel porter". And a friend told me he'd seen a sign outside a Hong Kong dentist: "Teeth extracted by the latest Methodists".

All of this goes to show how difficult it is for one human being to communicate clearly with another human being. And it's not just language that makes it difficult. It can be the way we stereotype each other. We make assumptions about the other person's attitudes and don't listen to what they're really saying.

People often misunderstand Jesus. "Gentle Jesus meek and mild" isn't the Jesus of the Bible. I see:

- **angry** Jesus who threw the moneychangers out of the Temple;
- **loving** Jesus who forgave the men who executed Him;
- **powerful** Jesus who brought healing and wholeness to so many people;
- **courageous** Jesus who confronted the corrupt establishment of His day.

That's *my* Jesus!

And people often make mistaken assumptions about Christian attitudes to things. For instance, because the Church considers homosexual acts to be sinful doesn't mean that the Church hates homosexuals. Far from it - because the Church is entirely populated by sinners, and our sins are no less intolerable to God. Perhaps, though, there *is* a difference. For the community of the church, whether the people in the pew, or ministers, or priests, or bishops, or archbishops or popes, are indeed sinners – but more importantly, we are *repentant* and *forgiven* sinners.

And that's no contradiction in terms.

FUEL PRICES

TUESDAY 12 SEPTEMBER 2000

I was working in London yesterday (and came back with a cold!) and got back to London Road Station earlier than I expected, a little after five o'clock. But I got home about the normal time. And the cause of the traffic delays was motorists queuing up for petrol. It brought back the time a little under thirty years ago when we suffered the "petrol crisis", and we sometimes had to queue for a couple of hours and even then, we only got a measly four gallons. The government even issued ration books to us all, though they never came into effect.

That time, it was the oil producers who caused the shortage. *This* time, it's the hauliers and farmers and taxi drivers and others who are blockading the refineries in order to impress on the government their view that it's the government's own fault for jacking up the price of fuel through excessive taxation.

Now (he said smugly) *I* filled up on Saturday before the crisis. I felt a bit like those wise maidens in the Bible who kept their lamps filled with oil so as to be ready if their bridegroom came to elope with them in the night. But my self-congratulation turned a bit sour when I found I had to pay £50 for a tankful that'll last me about a week. And about forty quid of that is tax.

The Bible tells Christians they must cheerfully pay taxes - even petrol taxes - properly levied by the government, because that's part of the government's job[60]. Of course, there's another side to that: government ministers will be accountable to God for how *just* they have been in their exercise of power. That's an awesome responsibility, and I hope that those we elect to govern us bear it in mind.

To finish, here's a story about a couple of nuns, who ran out of petrol one day out in the countryside. One of them trudged off to find a garage. When she found one, they didn't have a spare petrol can for her to use, but eventually the garage owner found the only container he had – an old potty his children had long ago grown out of. She filled it with a couple of litres of petrol and trudged carefully back to the car. She was just pouring from the potty into the tank when a farm hand passed by, driving a herd of cows. "I don't share your religion, sisters," he said, "but I certainly admire your faith!"

---

[60] See PAYING OUR FAIR WHACK earlier

WHICH SIDE ARE YOU ON?

WEDNESDAY 4 OCTOBER 2000

D id you see those pictures yesterday of our victorious Olympians returning from Sydney? Did you see them, proudly holding out their gold and silver and bronze medals? Did you see their *smiles*? As Katharine Merry, bronze medallist in the 400m, said: "You'll see a smile from us for a long time."

Did you see those other pictures? The picture of 12-year old Muhammad al-Durrah hiding behind his father

moments before four Israeli bullets smashed into his young body and ripped his life away?[61] And then his father is killed and an ambulance man trying to help is killed by more Israeli fusillades. These were scenes of utmost horror. To make it worse, the conflict was

---

[61] The Israeli Defence Force initially accepted responsibility for the death, but later claimed it had been staged by Palestinian militants. This does not explain the death of the father or the ambulanceman.

47

in Netzarim in the Gaza Strip, part of what we call the Holy Land. The blood of the fifty Palestinian dead this last week has defiled the very ground that Jesus once walked.

And the cause of the bloodshed is: who owns Jerusalem and the West Bank? Back in the mists of time, God gave the land to Abraham's children. You can read all about it in the 12th chapter of the book of Genesis. The trouble is that the Palestinians and the Israelis both claim descent from Abraham. They both claim to be Abraham's children, so both claim to own the land. And so they have fought for years, and they continue to fight.

So here's a question for you. What better represents the aspirations of the six billion people who populate the earth? Is it those who train and persevere and strive to do their best and maybe even achieve their goals through dedicated effort? Or is it those who turn to weapons to pursue their ends, who seek to obtain by force what their failure to negotiate denies them? In short, is it the hope**ful**, or the hope**less** who best represent humankind?

I know which side God is on. The apostle Paul sets it out quite neatly: *I keep working towards that day when I will finally be all that Christ Jesus saved me for and wants me to be. No, dear friends, I am still not all I should be, but I am focusing all my energies on this one thing: Forgetting the past and looking forward to what lies ahead, I strain to reach the end of the race and receive the prize for which God, through Christ Jesus, is calling us up to heaven.*[62] And the question I leave with you today is this: which side are you on? Are you looking back, or are you moving forward?

---

[62] Philippians 4:12b-14 NLT

PERSPECTIVES

FRIDAY 8 DECEMBER 2000

I've been delivering live *Thought for the Day* messages on Radio Leicester for many years now, and the brief for these is: to be topical. I usually wait until the previous evening and check the news headlines. Last night – and for various reasons I didn't get started on the job until 11 o'clock – I found a mish-mash of different stories that can be read in differing ways, according to your prejudices.

The European summit in Nice produces a whole crop of spin. The rapid reaction force - or the seeds of a European army? The Human rights convention - or the embryonic constitution of a super-state? Whether Germany should be more equal than the rest of the members – or whether Germany should have more votes because of its larger population? Not to mention the anarchists intent on disrupting the meeting, and the French gendarmerie intent on thwarting their violent protests.

And then there was the report that the number of speed cameras on Britain's roads is to double. An advance for road safety – or another jackbooted step towards a police state? And the saga of the American presidential election. Gore trying to steal the presidency from the rightful winner – or Bush trying to get into the White House by a corrupt electoral process?

So many different points of view, so many different spins. You pays your money (and aren't newspapers getting more and more expensive these days?) and you takes your choice.

But one story stands out as unspinnable. The killing of young Damilola Taylor in Peckham appalled the nation[63]. And yesterday, on what would have been his eleventh birthday, the church[64], whose Sunday School Damilola Taylor attended, hosted a memorial service for him. It was impossible not to have been deeply moved by the grief of Damilola's brother Tunde, as he spoke about the loveable and lively youngster whose life was so cruelly snatched from him. It was impossible not to respect Tunde's courage in admitting to his feelings of guilt for not having been there to protect his brother. And it was impossible not to applaud Tunde's deep Christian certainty that Damilola is resting in the arms of his LORD. In Tunde's simple nobility of grief lie the seeds of victory over the evil that brought about Damilola Taylor's death. It puts the rest of the news into perspective, doesn't it? The question is, what *really* matters – to you?

---

[63] There was an incompetent, if not corrupt, police investigation of the killing. After two failed trials, eventually in 2006 teenage brothers Ricky and Danny Preddie were convicted of manslaughter and given 8-year custodial sentences. Ricky was paroled in 2010 but recalled in 2011 for breach of conditions. Danny was paroled in 2011.

[64] Mountain of Fire and Miracles Ministries in Old Kent Road, London, a Pentecostal church. The MFM church in Lagos is the largest Nigerian church, attended by *100,000* people each Sunday! There is a branch in Leicester. Their mission statement includes the following: "Mountain of Fire and Miracles Ministries is a full gospel ministry devoted to the revival of apostolic signs, Holy Ghost fireworks and the unlimited power of God to deliver to the uttermost. [In MFM] absolute holiness within and without, as the greatest spiritual insecticide, and a condition for heaven is taught openly. MFM is a do-it-yourself gospel ministry where your hands are trained to wage war and your fingers to fight."

CELESTIAL SPLENDOUR

Tuesday 9 January 2001

D oesn't Christmas seem a long time ago? All that food, and now all those diets to make up for it! The cards from distant – and not-so-distant - friends and relatives have gone; the tree that looked so pretty shed its leaves and has been sent for recycling; the tinsel and glitter have been put away. And, following tradition, we took it all down on Twelfth Night, the same day that the Church remembers the journey of the wise men to worship the new-born Jesus.

The wise men saw something unprecedented in the sky – a star that moved and eventually stopped exactly where Jesus and his mother were living. This evening, if the sky is clear, we will be able to see – if not an unprecedented, at least a fairly unusual - event in the sky. There's to be a total eclipse of the moon. Clouds permitting, it will be a brilliant spectacle.

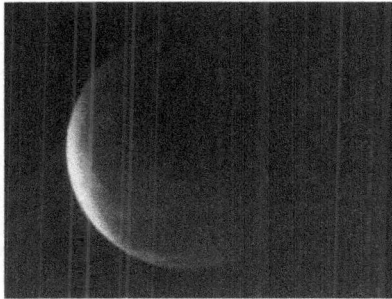

Isn't the night sky an awesome sight? Those uncountable numbers of galaxies; those trillions of stars in each galaxy; those unknowable numbers of planets and moons that revolve round them. And humankind sees the skies as something to reach out for, something that we want to investigate. There's enough romance in us to want to "boldly go" and explore the skies, just like the Starship Enterprise. Last week I explored some titchy hills on the Welsh borders, and I have to say that it wasn't so much a case of "to boldly go", more a case of "to oldly blow - and puff and pant and wheeze!" But I digress.

Here in Leicester we have the immense privilege of being home to the National Space Centre, soon to be completed. And even more exciting, there's the possibility that Mission Control for a Mars expedition will be run from here, if funds can be raised[65]. The Space Centre is a landmark for the spirit of hope and curiosity that God placed into the hearts of us human beings, and it is an honour for Leicester to be chosen as the focus of that endeavour.

You see, looking outwards, exploring, is absolutely necessary for humankind. We need a purpose, both in our individual lives, and as the human race. Space exploration, even if it's only with the naked eye, like the wise men, or tonight at the eclipse, fulfils part of God's design for us. As it says in the Bible: *Where there is no vision, the people perish.*[66]

---

[65] Eventually, it was – the Beagle 2 Mission. And it was a non-heroic failure. We don't even know if it landed on Mars or has tootled off into deep space. But at least, we tried.
[66] Proverbs 29:18 NIVUK

GOOD SAMARITANS
TUESDAY 6 FEBRUARY 2001

There are some things that just take your breath away. England's majestic Rugby win on Saturday afternoon was exhilarating[67]. Leicester City's win over Chelsea was no less inspiring. The achievement of solo round-the-world yachtswoman Ellen MacArthur in making up the deficit and getting close to the lead of the Vendée Globe race gladdens our hearts. Sporting accomplishments take us out of the everyday world for a little while and give us a glimpse of nobler things, of the spirit of human endeavour and the will to achieve.

But the best news of the last few days must be the amazing rescue of the middle-aged brother and sister, ten days after the terrible earthquake in Gujarat. Two people saved, against all the odds, yet an untold number – perhaps 30,000 (who knows?) – who died. It was providential for those two, with access to water and food under the rubble of their ruined apartment.

Can we imagine what it has been like for them since that mighty earthquake struck? Did their hopes of rescue dwindle away as day followed night followed day? Were they preparing themselves for an inevitable death when they heard movement above the ruins that trapped them? How their hopes must suddenly have been raised as the rescuers scraped away at the debris that entrapped them. And then, human contact at last! Voices, and faces, and strong arms to pull them free.

---

[67] England beat Wales 44-15 at the Millennium Stadium, Cardiff.

God loves all of His children, wherever and whoever they are. Jesus taught that God cares when even a sparrow dies, and reminded us that we are worth much more than a mere sparrow. God knows the very number of hairs on our heads, He cares so much[68]. Our loving Father grieves for the suffering of the people He created, and He knows every one by name, you and me and the victims in Gujarat.

And yet we so often feel helpless in the face of disaster, especially when that disaster is on the other side of the world. Few of us are able to go out and help directly. So what *can* we do? Obviously, we can give our money, however little, to the appeal launched by the Disasters Emergency Committee or perhaps through our place of worship. And we can pray for the relief of suffering and the provision of shelter and food and medicines and all the things the survivors need.

This is a time for us to be Good Samaritans.

---

[68] *What's the price of a pet canary? Some loose change, right? And God cares what happens to it even more than you do. He pays even greater attention to you, down to the last detail—even numbering the hairs on your head! So don't be intimidated by all this bully talk. You're worth more than a million canaries.* [Matthew 10:29-31 MSG]

THE TAG RUDDER

TUESDAY 6 MARCH 2001

The last three occasions I've brought a *Thought for the Day* I've found myself dealing with tragedy and disaster. I hoped that I'd be able to bring something more cheerful today, but a glance down the news just seems to bring more of the same. The Portuguese bridge disaster[69], the school shooting in America[70], floods in Mozambique, the terrorist bomb explosion outside the BBC Television Centre in London, and of course the continuing distress about Foot and Mouth Disease[71] fill the news programmes. And this is hot on the heels of the Gujarat earthquake, and a continual stream of murders, and political violence in all quarters of the world.

It's almost as if the whole nation – perhaps even the whole world – is afflicted by **S**easonal **A**ffective **D**isorder. You know, the depression and despair some people experience through the dark days of Winter, only relieved by the bright sunlight of Summer. We seem to be caught in a never-ending cycle of gloom, of tragedy, of disaster.

And we feel powerless to act in the face of all these things.

---

[69] The Hintze Ribeiro Bridge in Entre-os-Rios, Portugal, collapsed on 4 March 2001, killing 70 people.

[70] Two pupils were killed and thirteen wounded by 15 year old pupil Charles Andrew Williams at Santana High School in Santee, California on 5 March 2001.

[71] More than 2000 farms saw their cattle slaughtered during this epidemic. It is officially estimated that the total cost to the country of this epidemic was £8 billion by its end in October 2001.

But have you heard about the Tag Rudder? The very biggest ships – cruise liners and oil tankers - have massive rudders, some ten storeys high, to turn them. But even their enormously powerful motors are not enough to do the job. So they have a tag rudder - a small rudder – attached to the main rudder. The tiny tag rudder is turned. This causes the main rudder to move, turning the ship onto a new course. It is the initial small effort of the tag rudder that ultimately makes the ship change course.

Now we can't generally stop natural disasters. But we *can* do something to make things better, after the event. We *can* respect the farming community's request to keep away from the countryside until the Foot and Mouth epidemic is over. We *can* continue to give to the disaster relief appeals. We *can* get involved in Comic Relief fund-raising in the next couple of weeks. And we *can* pray about these things, and ask God's help in overcoming the consequences of these terrible calamities. Because God is not a remote force "out there", but is One who came to earth and lived among us, experiencing life, including its down sides of calamity and disaster - just like we do.

Your actions and your prayers might seem small, but they can have a disproportionate effect for the good.

But you have to make that first little effort.

FANTASY

FRIDAY 6 APRIL 2001

Leave it aht! After weeks of hype, the nation now knows it was Lisa wot dun it. Shot Phil Mitchell, that is. You know, the obnoxious bloke in *Eastenders*. Actually, the most obnoxious of the several obnoxious blokes in *Eastenders*, and lots of people thought he had it coming.

And the revelation that it was Lisa has been in the news on BBC and ITV, and a football match was put back by 15 minutes so viewers wouldn't miss its start because they were glued to the telly[72]. There's even been a forensic analysis of the case by former deputy chief constable John Stalker.

It seems that fiction increasingly overtakes fact in the way the media reports soap storylines. Many people are more interested in the lives of soap opera characters than in the real lives of their work colleagues or neighbours. When Grace Archer died in an episode of *The Archers* on the wireless in the mid-fifties, the BBC was inundated with wreaths and floral tributes from heartbroken listeners to the Home Service. And, do you remember, even Tony Blair was moved to appeal in public for the release of Deirdre from *Corrie*[73] from an unjust prison sentence? The tabloid papers seem increasingly unable to distinguish between the fictional

---

[72] Liverpool v Barcelona, UEFA Cup semi-final, which Liverpool went on to win.

[73] *Coronation Street*, the ITV chief soap opera.

characters and the actors who portray them. The cult of celebrity merges them into a blurry hybrid.

I guess a little bit of fantasy does no harm, so long as we don't get it out of perspective. Most of us have romantic flights of fancy about ourselves. Apparently, a common daydream among young girls is to faint in the street and be resuscitated by Prince William who happens to be passing by, and then swept up in his manly arms to life as his Princess in Windsor Castle[74]. Men - perhaps including Prince William - often fantasize about heroically saving someone's life.

This Sunday is Palm Sunday, the start of what Christians call Holy week, leading up to Easter. On Palm Sunday, we remember the crowds lining the streets as Jesus rode into Jerusalem, cheering and applauding this celebrity whom they thought would become their warrior-king to liberate them from Roman oppression. But they were cheering a fantasy, for Jesus wasn't coming to Jerusalem to be proclaimed King. The reality was harder, and harsher.

Jesus had no romantic illusions. Injustice and death lay ahead of him. And unlike Phil Mitchell, Jesus didn't deserve it. But, even so, Jesus prayed for his killers: "Father, forgive them. They don't know what they're doing".

Sorted.

True.

---

[74] This was two years before the Prince met Catherine Middleton, so at the time of broadcast, there was still hope.

HOW TO VOTE
FRIDAY 11 MAY 2001

So it's day four of the General Election campaign. From now to polling day, we're going to be bombarded with party political broadcasts and leaflets through our doors. The political journalists will dominate our news and current affairs programmes, and there are going to be countless interviews and debates. One party has already published its manifesto and all the others will be announced in the next few days. Every candidate and every party is going to make promises about what they will do if we'll only vote for them. Our job is to decide: will they fulfil those promises?

Politicians, it is said, are held in very low esteem by the public. Politicians themselves have always been cynical about their profession. The Greek politician Themistocles wrote around 470 BC "If you showed me two roads, one to Hell and one to politics, I'd choose the one to Hell every time". And even Winston Churchill was a bit jaundiced about politics. Someone asked him what was the main qualification for being a politician. He replied, "The ability to foretell what is going to happen tomorrow, next week, next month and next year – and the ability afterwards to explain why it didn't happen."

Whether we want it or not, we have an important duty come polling day. We have the right to help choose the person we want to be our representative in parliament. We have the right to influence the policies that will govern the country over the next few years. People struggled and some died to win us the right to vote, and we have a responsibility to use our vote wisely.

So what qualities should we look for in choosing which candidate to vote for? The Bible outlines the qualities that God expects of Christian leaders. Many, I suggest, should apply when we're choosing our MPs. The leader, says the Bible, must be *above reproach ... faithful to their partner ... temperate, self-controlled, respectable, hospitable, persuasive, not given to excessive wine, gentle rather than violent, not quarrelsome, not a lover of money ... have a well organised personal life, be of good reputation, and be sincere and worthy of respect*[75].

That's a pretty tall order! How many of us measure up? But we *are* entitled to expect more of our politicians than we are of ourselves. For after all, we give them, for a time, great power over us. Let *us* choose politicians with those good biblical qualities, and let *them* exercise those good personal qualities as *they* govern *us*.[76]

---

[75] 1 Timothy 3:2-4, 8 my paraphrase

[76] There was a remarkable sequel to this talk. Election agents for three Parties - Conservatives, Labour and Liberal-Democratic - each in a different Leicestershire constituency, complained to the BBC that in this talk, I had singled out their candidate unfairly. Each particularly pointed to the phrase *faithful to their partner* as the unfair phrase, among the others. Of course, I had singled out none of them. A senior BBC Regional executive replied that as the three main political parties had equally taken offence, the BBC's duty to remain unbiased in the run-up to an election had been amply demonstrated. And that in any case, there was no bias in what I had said. You wouldn't think that politicians were so thin-skinned, would you? Or so promiscuous. And so guilt-laden.

ON BEING HUMAN

TUESDAY 12 JUNE 2001

It's an exciting time in Leicestershire right now, at least architecturally. Leicester City have lined everything up and they're about to start work on the new larger football stadium. It's been a saga of more stops than starts so far, but at last the Foxes are going to have a stadium worthy of their Premier status in this 21st Century. The National Space Centre is almost ready to open its doors.

What a privilege for our City to have the best space facility in Europe, and what an opportunity for jobs and tourism! And Conkers, the new Centre in the National Forest, with its building a strong contender for European Building of the year, recently opened. Three fine public buildings befitting a county that has had more than its share of architectural disasters over the years.

The National Space Centre
a.k.a. "the maggot"

It's not so much the good and interesting buildings that have been demolished as the tawdry cheapjack buildings that so often replaced them that have diminished the cityscape. It is important for people to be proud of their environment, and buildings matter. But people need to feel a sense of ownership of public buildings

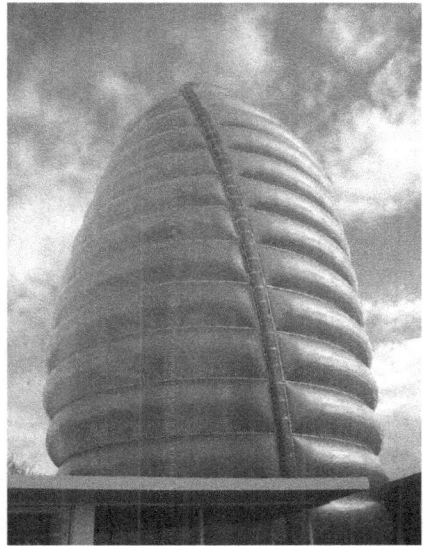

too. You don't spray your own wall with graffiti; you don't break your own windows; you don't uproot trees you've planted yourself. Good buildings give us a sense of nobler things.

Too many of us feel cut off from the privileges and responsibilities of citizenship. That's partly why the voting turn-out last Thursday was the lowest for 82 years[77]. "What's the point? It's nothing to do with me. *I* don't count."

However, the Bible reveals that we are uniquely valuable to God. He had each one of us in mind right from the first pico-second of the Big Bang, when He said "Let there be light". And because He could see how we stumble around making a mess of things, He sent Jesus to show us the way to lives overflowing with happiness. A key teaching is to care for each other, even people who are our enemies. The Good Samaritan, who looked after the man who had been mugged, came from an enemy nation.

Last week it was reported that Mazen Joulani, 33, a Muslim pharmacist, was shot dead in Jerusalem, probably in revenge for the suicide bomb that had killed 21 Israelis in Tel Aviv. And his family donated his organs to the Israeli transplant system for transplant, and three Jewish lives were saved as a result.

That's true nobility – and Jesus would approve.

---

[77] Turnout was 59% of the electorate, the lowest turnout since 1918's "Coupon Election", in which property-owning women over 30 years old had the vote for the first time, as did men over 21 who were resident householders.

RÔLE MODELS

WEDNESDAY 11 JULY 2001

Isn't the news boring at the moment? Perhaps I desperately need my holiday. Yesterday's top story was about the Tory MPs' initial votes for the five candidates to replace William Hague as leader of the party[78]. And the other "big news" was that Helen and Josh have been nominated for eviction from the Big Brother[79] house. Which gave me an idea. Why don't the Tory grandees put their five candidates into the Big Brother household and we can all vote them out one by one over the coming weeks? It might spice things up a bit!

I can't ever remember being bored when I was a youngster. Even those long summer holidays seemed full of sunshine and fun. Perhaps it's just that I'm so much older, and much more jaundiced about the world.

---

[78] Hague was ousted because the Conservatives failed to make progress at the June 2001 general election. Hague was the first Conservative leader since Austen Chamberlain (d. 1937) not to have become Prime Minister.

[79] Big Brother was at the time a popular television reality show. A dozen or so "housemates" lived together in a "house" and were under television surveillance 24 hours a day, and were given various (usually inane) tasks to perform. One by one, the housemates would be nominated for eviction by their fellow housemates, and the public would vote by telephone as to which would be publicly evicted from the house each Friday. The housemates would continually say that they were bored.

But I did notice one news item that cheered me up no end. Dan Dare is making a comeback, this time in an animated TV series. I remember, when I was about 9 years old, waiting impatiently for the *Eagle* comic to be delivered. And I would drop everything and avidly turn to Dan Dare,

Mekon

Pilot of the Future. And as I followed the story, I *became* Dan Dare, flying my spacecraft and defeating my arch-enemy, the Mekon - who, I now realise, bears an uncanny resemblance to the aforesaid William Hague.

And at other times, I became "Just" William Brown, the Scarlet Pimpernel, Biggles, Rob Roy MacGregor (well, I *am* half Scottish), Jennings, Ivanhoe, and Robin Hood. I developed a bit of a 10-year-old's crush on Patricia Driscoll, who played Maid Marian, and it wasn't long after that when I forsook the *Eagle* for the more grown-up delights of *Reveille*, and I guess that marked the ending of my childhood.

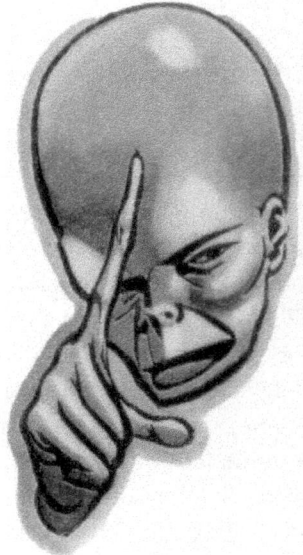

Hague

Even as adults, we need rôle models, someone to whose good character we aspire. But even our heroes and heroines are simply human beings, with all the flaws and foibles of mankind.

Christians believe though, that one person, and one person only, had none of those flaws, none of those foibles. Whether you're a follower of Jesus or not, his life and His teaching show Him as a rôle model worth following.

He taught two basic rules: Love God with everything you've got; and love your neighbour as much as you love yourself.[80] If you do, He promised that we would have life, and have it to the full.

And that ain't boring!

---

[80] *One of the teachers of the law came and heard them debating. Noticing that Jesus had given them a good answer, he asked him, Of all the commandments, which is the most important? The most important one, answered Jesus, is this: 'Hear, O Israel, the Lord our God, the Lord is one. Love the Lord your God with all your heart and with all your soul and with all your mind and with all your strength.' The second is this: 'Love your neighbour as yourself.' There is no commandment greater than these.* [Mark 12:27-31 NIVUK]

IMMORTALITY

FRIDAY 10 AUGUST 2001

I'll bet I know some things that you don't know. For instance, today is the anniversary of the birth of some people who were very important, at least in their own back yard. Happy birthday to John the Blind, King of Bohemia in 1296; Peterus I Scheemaeckers, a Flemish tomb stone sculptor, in 1652; the composer Franz Joseph Leonti Meyer von Schavensee in 1720; Michail M Soschtschenko, the Russian author, in 1895; Arthur Porritt of New Zealand, who won a 1924 Olympic bronze medal in the 100 metres and was born this day in 1900; Fred Ridgway, the England fast bowler born in 1923; and Keisha Delancy, Miss Turks & Caicos Islands 1996 and Miss Universe 1997, born in 1973.

And on this day, we remember the deaths of Erik IV Plovpenning, King of Denmark, who was murdered in 1250; Kinjikitile "Bokero" Ngwale, the East African rebel leader, hanged in 1905; Ivor Dean, British actor in 1974; and Arias Arnulfo, 3 time president of Panama, in 1988, among many others.

I told you you wouldn't know about them. To be honest with you, I hadn't the faintest idea of the existence of any of these people until I looked up what happened today in history. Nary a one of them means anything to me at all.

Yet, every one of these people had a mother and a father who loved them. I don't know if they had children, but if they did, no doubt those children loved them too. And they had friends who cared about them and who were saddened when they died. And their children and their friends remembered them and perhaps told *their* children and *their* friends about them. And so the memories of these people, and what they were like, and what they did, was passed down until – well, there's *me* telling *you* about them. And that's a sort of immortality.

One of God's commandments – one of His rules, if you like - is to *honour your father and your mother*[81]. And that includes remembering them after they have gone. Few of us will go down in the history books, but we *will* be remembered.

What sort of person will your family and friends remember you as? Dearly loved, or soon forgotten?

The apostle Paul said: *Remember this: Whoever sows sparingly will also reap sparingly, and whoever sows generously will also reap generously*[82].

---

[81] Exodus 20:12 NIVUK
[82] 2 Corinthians 9:6 NIVUK

9/11

*T*hought for the Day here on Radio Leicester is supposed to reflect on some current item of news. And there is still only one item that dominates every bulletin and current affairs programme and newspaper. The terrorist outrages of 11th September in New York and Washington and Philadelphia have shaken everyone[83]. Friends and family and colleagues in several countries have been in touch with me by e-mail and phone. They tell me that there is the same shock where they are as we feel here, and the same incomprehension, and the same fear. Which is exactly what the perpetrators of these crimes hoped would happen.

And the story is not yet over. Even though the Mayor of New York has said there is virtually no hope of finding any remaining survivors, there are still people clinging to the faint hope that their loved one will be found alive. The United States, the most formidably armed nation in the world, is trying to create a united world front against terrorism, while apparently preparing to wreak a terrible

---

[83] On 11 September 2001, 19 al-Qaeda terrorists hijacked four commercial passenger jet airliners. Two were deliberately crashed into the "Twin Towers" of the World Trade Center in New York, one was crashed into the Pentagon, and the fourth crashed into a field in Philadelphia after some of the passengers tried to wrest control of the aircraft from the hijackers, which the hijackers were aiming at the Capitol Building in Washington DC. 2977 people from more than 90 countries were killed altogether, plus the 19 terrorists.

retribution against those who aid and shelter the foes of democracy.

As I speak, there are so many unanswered questions. Will the rulers of Afghanistan extradite Osama bin Laden to the Americans? What will the Americans do with him if he is handed over? What form will the war against terrorism take? What will be the reaction of the terrorist groups: will we see the launch of a bitter campaign of terror against the peoples of the democracies? What will be the effect of all this on relations between the various racial and religious communities in this country and abroad? We certainly live in uncertain times.

Right now, many people feel frightened, tossed about on the stormy waves of uncharted waters. Many generations of humanity have experienced similar feelings: in times of war, and famine and plague. And like them, we can turn to the words of Scripture for comfort. Two and half thousand years ago, a psalm was written. It starts like this:

> *God is our refuge and strength,*
> *always ready to help in times of trouble.*
> *So we will not fear when earthquakes come*
> *and the mountains crumble into the sea.*

And it ends with these words of affirmation and assurance:

> *The LORD of Heaven's Armies is here among us;*
> *the God of Israel is our fortress.*[84]

---

[84] Psalm 46:1-2, 11 NLT

WORDS (AGAIN)

FRIDAY 26 OCTOBER 2001

I've always thought of myself as more argute than an apple-knocker, although I do confess to being prone to lollygagging, and I really hope I'm not a toplofty. Maybe you think I'm a blatherskite but I'd deny any accusation of being a doryphor. If all of this gives you horripilation, then I'd say you were atrabilious.

"What *is* he on about?", I hear you ask. Well, the good folk who publish the Oxford English Dictionary are publishing a list of some Weird and Wonderful Words that we've stopped using. They suggest that these are both useful and interesting words that are ripe for a come-back. So when I say I'm argute, I'm shrewd; an apple-knocker is an ignoramus, lollygagging is laziness, and a toplofty is an arrogant man. A blatherskite is someone who talks nonsense and a doryphor is a pedantic critic. Horripilation is when the hairs on the back of your arms stand up through fear, cold or excitement, and atrabilious means bad tempered.

Aren't these delicious words, ripe to roll around your mouth? I have a private store of words of my own that I hope one day I'll be able to make use of. One is "myristicivorous" meaning "feeding upon nutmegs", and another is "eleemosynary" which means "connected to the giving of alms".

It's funny how words go out of fashion. When I was a lad, I was severely told off if I used the swear word "ruddy", but I haven't heard it used for ages. And did anyone else with a cold get dosed with "ipecacuanha wine, syrup of squills and glycerine"?

There's another word we hear less and less these days. There's been a spate of announcements in Parliament recently, with several ministers correcting things they've said, or explaining why unwelcome announcements have been published at a time when everyone's attention has been elsewhere. The missing word in most of these statements has been "sorry".

Sorry is a little word that means a lot yet is incredibly hard to say. Sorry is a powerful word. Sorry can restore relationships. Sorry can increase the sum total of human happiness. I wonder if there's someone *you* need to say sorry to.

Christians know that saying sorry to God is the first step in restoring our relationship with Him. It's even got a special theological word, it's so important. We call it **repentance**. This means thinking again, turning away from wrong things, making a fresh start. And whenever someone repents and asks for forgiveness, the Bible tells us that the angels in heaven throw a party.

So saying sorry to God can make the welkin ring. (Oh yes - the "welkin" means the "heavens"!)

TOMORROW, AND TOMORROW, AND TOMORROW[85]

Well, oo-er! Our Prime Minister[86] has got a blind spot about spelling the word "tomorrow". He spells the "to" bit with two Os. At least he did – three times - in a personal letter that got into the news.

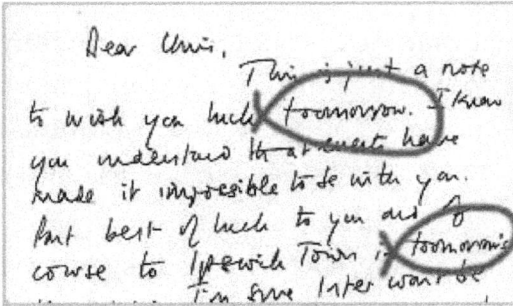

Whoops! Actually "tomorrow" is one of the most commonly mis-spelt words. Poor old Tony.

I wouldn't want to exagerrate, but it's neccesary to point out that it's definately an embarassment to get the beggining of the word "tommorow" wrong. That's six of the most difficult words. Spot them? Spell them? Exaggerate; necessary; definitely; embarrassment; beginning; tomorrow. And can anyone tell me the right way to spell "withhold"? One H or two, it never looks right!

Spellings are only wrong when they flout a convention. There is no law about it. We spell "colour" with a U, but our American cousins get on perfectly well without it.

---

[85] Shakespeare: *The Tragedy of Macbeth*, Act 5, Scene 5
[86] The Rt. Hon Anthony Charles Lynton Blair PC, MP, educ. The Chorister School, Durham; Fettes College, Edinburgh; St John's College, Oxford. Who may all be ashamed of his performance in this matter.

What about bough, cough, dough, lough, and rough? All of 'em spelled with o-u-g-h. There's no logic.

Words, even beautiful sounding words, can sometimes pose a problem. When I was about ten or eleven years old, I concluded I would never get to heaven. The reason was that I used to read the Authorised or King James Version of the Bible, translated into 16th Century English. And I used to love the sound of the language, and all the "thees" and "thines" and "begats" and "behoveths", which amounted to something like a secret code that I loved to try to crack. A verse in Mark's gospel really threw me, though. It said *Verily I say unto you, Whosoever shall not receive the kingdom of God as a little child, he shall not enter therein.*[87] Well, I was no longer a little child, and I hadn't received the Kingdom of God while I was a little child, so it was too late, or so I thought. I had understood the little word "as" to mean "while".

But translated into modern English, the verse says, *I tell you the truth, anyone who will not receive the kingdom of God like a little child will never enter it.*[88] **Like** a little child, not **while** a little child. Hallelujah! I was allowed in!

So it's not too late for anyone to come into the kingdom of God. All it needs is the simple trusting accept-it-at-face-value faith of a little child. No quibbles about the spelling or the grammar, no discussion about the logic, just an acceptance of God's love.

How about receiving the kingdom today? For tomorrow never comes.

---

[87] Mark 10:15 KJV
[88] Mark 10:15 NIVUK

JENNIFER JANE BROWN

TUESDAY 8 JANUARY 2002

Not even the hardest of hearts can have failed to be moved by the news of the death of little Jennifer Jane Brown. Less than two weeks ago, we saw Gordon Brown, the "Iron Chancellor", a man not generally given to public displays of emotion, bursting with joy as he announced that at the age of 50 he had become a father for the first time. And we heard him say the same thing that every father says on the birth of his child, that she was the most beautiful baby in the world. And every father is right.

And Sarah and Gordon Brown knew and loved Jennifer Jane not just for the few days since her birth, but for many months previously. They noticed the signs of life, the kicks and movements as she exercised herself in the womb. They planned and prepared for Jennifer Jane's arrival. They took delight in choosing her names; they set aside a nursery for her; they bought clothes and cots and pushchairs. They even speculated about the long term future of their daughter.

But tiny Jennifer Jane was born very prematurely, and needed highly skilled medical care, which she indeed received. Despite this, last night, Jennifer Jane lost her fight for life and died in her parents' arms. That will be some small comfort for Gordon and Sarah Brown, who must be feeling empty and lost this morning. They will be asking that ultimate question: "Why?". And the only answer Christians can give is that we don't know, but that God has His reasons that they will understand one day when they are reunited with Jennifer Jane in heaven.

There will be further comfort for the Browns through their own Christian faith. Jennifer Jane was Christened at their request a day previously as an act surrendering her to the tender care of God. In God's infinite love, He took baby Jennifer Jane back. The Browns will take consolation in the sure knowledge that she is cradled in the loving arms of God the Father of us all.

We don't usually do this on Thought for the Day, but will you join me in this short prayer?[89]

> Loving God, we are conscious how fragile is the thread that separates life from death, and how suddenly it can be broken. We ask You to help us remember, that on both sides of that divide we are surrounded by Your love. Bring comfort to all who mourn this morning, we ask. Amen

---

[89] This *Thought* brought an astonishing response. Radio Leicester had several dozen telephone calls, and I received many letters thanking me for dealing with such a sad and sensitive subject. I issued about 20 copies of the prayer in response to listener requests.

WORDS (YET AGAIN)

TUESDAY 5 FEBRUARY 2002

Collins' new dictionary has just been published together with its predictions as to the best word newcomer for the year 2002. Their top contenders are "In Silico" which refers to computer programming, and "Pink Viagra", which I won't go into this early in the day. They've been doing that since 1902, when the word they predicted was Teddy-Bear. I guess they got that right. They got "manic depression" right, too, in 1905. But at various times they predicted other words that signally failed the test of time. Who remembers "bovrilize" meaning to condense, or "groceteria" now superseded by "supermarket"?

Words also change their meanings over time. "Economist" used to mean someone who was thrifty, but now it means someone who claims to know all about wealth and its creation and distribution. And today's "pundit" is someone who bores television viewers with his ten-a-penny, saloon-bar opinions about football, whereas it used to mean a wise and learned man.

Words, of course, are very important. They can have unexpected force, provoking strong reactions in the hearer. A Blairite utterance (oh yes, "Blairite" is a word that crept into the language in 2000) - anyway, the Prime Minister used the word "wreckers" in a speech to his supporters last weekend. And the assembled comradely brothers and sisters took great umbrage at what they took to be a slur against their good selves.

Christians know the power of words. The Bible describes the development of the universe as happening, era by era, day by day, at God's spoken commands. *Let there be light*[90] starts the chain of events, and on the sixth day *Let us make man in our image, in our likeness*[91]. Words have power. Indeed, the central figure of Christianity - Jesus Christ Himself - is called "The Word" in the Bible[92].

The Apostle James warned that words can be a dangerous thing. Our tongues can run away with us and get us into trouble[93]. Have you ever said the wrong thing to someone? Spoken to someone in such a way that you've hurt them, even if you didn't mean it? Or passed on gossip and rumour and untrue stories about someone? And then it's so hard to put things right. Even if you apologise straight away, you're left feeling that the apology sounds thin, that they're thinking, "He really meant that". And you feel guilty and ashamed.

That's why words can be dangerous: you can so easily end up digging a hole for yourself. Bad words rebound on you. But so do good ones.

So how about saying something nice to someone today? Maybe niceness will rebound on *you*.

---

[90] Genesis 1:3 MOST TRANSLATIONS
[91] Genesis 1:26 NIVUK
[92] E.g. John 1:1 ALL TRANSLATIONS
[93] The whole of the letter from James is permeated with this thought.

ME FIRST

TUESDAY 5 MARCH 2002

B ad things have been happening locally recently. Outbreaks of vandalism, for instance in Mountsorrel and South Wigston. There was an appalling robbery at a store in Wymeswold by vicious and heedless hoodlums who nearly succeeded in burning the store down with the helpless owner inside it. How can people do these things?

We live in a "me" culture, where society tells us our primary consideration is to look after our own interests. The advertising thrust daily at us teaches us gratification is ours from the products we buy; we can buy recklessly and then pay off our debts over 20 years at virtually nothing each month; that our health can be maintained or improved by taking this packaged exercise programme or following that diet. If we buy the clothes and sportswear modelled by Posh and Becks[94], then somehow we take on the glamour of their fame and fortune. Or at least that's what Big Business wants us to feel.

The concentration on "me first" leads us to forget our responsibility to others. Concepts of duty and loyalty, care and concern, come a poor second. But Jesus Christ told the famous story of the Good Samaritan, emphasising our common humanity, and He made it clear we have a duty to love our neighbour as much as we love ourselves.

---

[94] A "celebrity couple": David Beckham, footballer, and his wife Victoria, known as "Posh" Spice of the Spice Girls singing group.

The vandal cares nothing for the consequences of his actions. The robber is unmindful of the devastation he wreaks on his terrified victim. He is a "me" person, not a "we" person. But what about *our* responsibilities? Do we care about the inhumanity of our prison system that forces teenage prisoners to slop out[95] each morning? Do we care about the exploitation of poor workers in poor countries, denied a fair and living wage by the companies that sell us our tea and coffee and chocolate and diamonds? Do we care about the treatment of the Al-Qaida prisoners held in Camp X-Ray under austere conditions? Do we care about the fate of those who dare to oppose President Mugabe of Zimbabwe?

Pastor Martin Niemöller was imprisoned because he opposed Hitler and the Nazis. He wrote this:

Martin Niemöller

> *First they came for the Jews and I did not speak out because I was not a Jew. Then they came for the Communists and I did not speak out because I was not a Communist. Then they came for the trade unionists and I did not speak out because I was not a trade unionist. Then they came for me and there was no one left to speak out for me.*

Yes, other people matter.

---

[95] Where WCs are not installed, prisoners have to make use of a bucket overnight and then carry them to a sluice room to empty them before breakfast.

Published: Tue, 5 Mar 2002 02:00:00 UTC

Prisons chief condemns 'degrading' conditions

The new chief inspector of prisons has warned that a prison wing where sanitation falls short of acceptable standards must clean up its act or face demolition.

Ann Owers said that Exeter prison will have to raise standards or face demolishing a wing where prisoners are still "slopping out".

Her report into D wing, which houses a disproportionate number of young prisoners with mental health problems, finds that conditions remain "degrading" for many occupants.

"D Wing should be demolished unless appropriate installation of integral sanitation is carried out," says her report.

Whilst the chief inspector welcomes progress made since the last inspection, she said that issues involving the health centre and D Wing "should be addressed as a matter of urgency".

Martin Narey, the director general of the Prison Service, said significant progress had been made at the jail.

"I am confident that many of the issues that concern the chief inspector in her latest report are currently being addressed," he said.

RENAMING

WEDNESDAY 3 APRIL 2002

So Leicester City's wonderful new stadium has got a name. The proposed "Walkers Bowl"[95] might take a bit of getting used to after over a century of "Filbert Street". Will Filbert Fox trot happily across to Freemens Wharf, like the wily urban fox he is? Or will there be a new mascot to match the new stadium and – possibly – the new league in the new season? What would we call him? For naming *things* is as important – and difficult – as naming babies.

The transport authorities are all at sea. The shipping forecast area Finisterre has been renamed Fitzroy. Lloyds List has started referring to ships as "it" instead of "she". And recently Liverpool Airport became John Lennon Airport. Incidentally, are there any *aerodromes* left these days?

We've just celebrated Easter Sunday, the climax of the Easter story. There's a little footnote in the Bible account. It tells of Judas Iscariot, who betrayed Jesus, hanging himself in remorse for his treachery. And the money he had been corrupted with was used to buy a claypit called the Potter's Field outside Jerusalem, and it was made into a cemetery for criminals and suicides. And the authorities renamed it *Akeldama*, the Field of Blood. It's said that Judas Iscariot was

---

[96] This, ahem, inspired idea was quietly dropped in the face of vast opposition from the good people of Leicestershire. However, in 2010, the club was sold to a Thai consortium "Asia Football Investments" fronted by the duty-free retailers King Power Group. The stadium is now officially called "The King Power Stadium".

the first to be buried there. Just another unfortunate death in the Holy Land.

And over this Easter weekend, things have gone horribly wrong in that same Holy Land. There have been other unfortunate deaths there, and people being horribly wounded also. What the Palestinian suicide bombers think they are achieving escapes me. And what the Israeli government thinks *it* is achieving by its massive retaliation is just as mysterious. To cap the horror of the situation, the latest focus of conflict is the small city of Bethlehem. The same Bethlehem that was the birthplace of Jesus, the Prince of Peace. Jesus, who once wept over Jerusalem, must be weeping over Bethlehem, and Ramallah, and all of the Holy Land.

I wish I understood the conflict in the Holy Land. I wish a simple solution could be found. There is too much history, and too much pride, and too many outside vested interests to make for a quick peace. Only the God that Arabs worship, and Jews worship, and Christians worship can do that. Let us pray to Him for a lasting and sensible reconciliation, for a softening of hard hearts, and a renaming of aspirations.

MAY DAY INNOCENCE

WEDNESDAY 1 MAY 2002

It's the First of May – May Day. I remember in the distant days of my childhood, the school Maypole was brought out and we danced and hopped in and out, led by the May Queen we had chosen, interweaving the coloured ribbons until the pole was braided. We sang a May song:

> Round and round the maypole, merrily we go,
> Tripping, tripping lightly, singing as we go.
> O, the happy pastime, on the village green,
> Dancing in the sunshine - hooray for the Queen!

Do they still dance round the Maypole, carefree boys and girls, following in the footsteps of generations of others? Do young maidens still go out at dawn to wash their faces in the May dew, to ensure that they shall have a beautiful complexion for the rest of the year?

For May Day is the traditional start of high summer, a day that for centuries was given over to revelry and carousing. In 1644, the Puritans banned the merrymaking, so licentious had the festivities become; but then, the Puritans were fond of banning anything that brought pleasure to the drab lives of the people.

May Day became a worker's festival in the late 1800s and even America celebrates it as Labor Day. The Catholic Church beat everyone to it, and proclaimed today as the Day of St Joseph the Worker twenty years earlier.

And today, the innocence of May Day has been hijacked by people who are going to demonstrate against what they see as the evils of global capitalism. Our TV screens are going to show footage of riot and mayhem this evening, with a hardcore of self-proclaimed anarchists signed up to engage in violent protest. And they will achieve nothing positive, though there will be injury to people and damage to property.

It was while musing on these matters, that I chanced across a couple of anniversaries whose conjunction made me smile, although I don't quite know why. For today is the fifth anniversary of Mr Blair being made Prime Minister; and it is the 50th anniversary of the creation of Mr Potato Head. There's no resemblance, but it's still funny.

But I chanced across something deep as well. The great evangelist and preacher George Whitefield wrote this in his diary in 1740 on this day: *Lord, show that Thou dost love me, by humbling and keeping me humble as long as I live. The means I leave to Thee.*

Maybe the May Day demonstrators could do with a bit of that.

I know I do.

MISTAKES

TUESDAY 28 MAY 2002

I used to work with Mike, a brilliant salesman and a great storyteller, who had one small problem: he had great difficulty in remembering peoples' names. He claimed once that someone suggested he try the technique of inventing a mental picture of something that mirrored the name. Apparently, he visited a potential customer called Mr Quakenbusch. He applied the technique. He pictured a little duck sitting under a bush. A few weeks later, there was a new product launch, and Mike proudly introduced his new customer to the Group Chairman. "Sir George," he said, "I'd like you to meet Mr. Duckshade." Fortunately, Mr Quakenbusch had a sense of humour and didn't mind Mike's mistake.

Yesterday, the Bank of England was forced to suspend the issue of its new, super-secure £5 note when it discovered that serial numbers could be rubbed off. Just the feature a forger delights in! It looks like someone made a big mistake in the specifications or the printing.

We all make mistakes of course. Some big, some small. That's part of being human. The person who never made a mistake never made anything, so it's said. We've all heard of the record companies that turned the Beatles down in 1960 because "the craze for guitar bands is over". And Alexander Graham Bell saw a great future for his invention, the telephone. *The day will come*, he said, *when every major city will have one.*

David was a great hero of the Old Testament. He killed the giant Goliath, and later on became King of Israel, revered for his poetry and music and his military and political prowess. Despite this, David made a big mistake. He committed adultery with Bathsheba, the wife of one of his generals[97]. David connived to send the general into a heated battle, and then withdrew all support, and the general was killed. This was to cover up the fact that Bathsheba was pregnant by David. And like most adulterous affairs, the result was misery. Bathsheba's baby died, and David nearly lost the throne.

But David asked God to forgive him for his sins, and God responded, and the kingdom was secure. Just as Jesus taught his disciples to pray, many centuries later: *forgive us our sins, just as we forgive those who sin against us.*

It's a two-way thing: forgive and be forgiven. And maybe then we can echo David's cry; *Create in me a pure heart, O God, and renew a steadfast spirit within me*[98].

---

[97] This part of David's story is told in 2 Samuel 11.
[98] Psalm 51:10 NIVUK

WORLD CUP

12 June 2002

There's no escaping the Football World Cup. If last Friday's match is anything to go by, 17 million of us will watch England play Nigeria this morning. That's one in three of the population. What the other two-thirds are up to, I don't know. But don't try ringing *me* during the match, 'cause I won't be answering the phone until after the final whistle!

What is it about football at this level that rouses such deep feelings for our national teams? Some people say that team sport is ritualised warfare. I suppose it's better to hoof a bag of wind around a field for 90 minutes than to lob missiles at one another. Others see a displaced religion in the game. Certainly there are some similarities to Christian observance. Where do large crowds gather to sing and chant? Churches and football grounds. Where do large crowds raise their hands in the air in exultation? Churches and football grounds. Where do people gather to express their collective aspirations, their feelings, their emotions? Churches and football grounds.

But of course the resemblance is only superficial. Bread and wine is not the same as pies and Bovril. The adulation of our footballing heroes falls short of worship. And all our footballers can do is play football to the limit of their ability. And they give us delight when they show their skills, and satisfaction when they win on our behalf. They also bring despair and disappointment when the team loses. But our God, the creator and sustainer of the universe, our loving Father, *He* is without limits. He gives us delight and satisfaction. And He never brings despair and disappointment.

Before every match in the World Cup, they play the National Anthems of the countries involved. I've been struck by how many are hymns, asking God to bless their country.

Perhaps one of the noblest sentiments is in our own National Anthem. Most of us only know the first verse, but listen to the third:

Not in this land alone,
But be God's mercies known,
From shore to shore!
Lord make the nations see,
That men should brothers be,
And form one family,
The wide world o'er.

And isn't that what this World Cup should be all about? The brotherhood of our common humanity? Because we are all God's children, and like every human father, God loves to see His children at play.

Ato, Kaz and Nik
official mascots for the
2002 FIFA World Cup

TRAVEL

MONDAY 15 JULY 2002

If you're on your way to work in your car as you are listening to Radio Leicester this morning, you're probably noticing that your journey is a bit easier than usual. The traffic is flowing more smoothly than normal. The queues at junctions are shorter. There are no traffic jams outside schools. No school crossing warden is protecting children from the vehicles rushing past. For school's out. The holidays have started. Teacher friends have been expectantly counting down the days to the end of term, and I guess some mums and dads have been counting down the same days with a little less enthusiasm.

Although the July fortnight is – in my view, sadly – a thing of the past, many families will be taking their annual holiday right now. It's more likely to be sangria in Seville than shandy in Skegness these days. Nowadays, travel is so easy and relatively cheap that people are taking their holidays in all corners of the world. My own son Christopher used up his holidays by spending the whole of June in Japan, following the World Cup – and he says it was a month-long party out there. The world is truly a smaller place.

And what an opportunity travel offers to experience different cultures and ways of life. I suppose this doesn't apply if all you want out of a holiday is a day sunbathing and a night in the clubs - pink and drink, no need to think – but for those willing to explore, what fascinating things there are to learn.

Of course, some people get blasé about travel. I well remember the old joke in Lupino Lane's[99] repertoire: "I went on a cruise round the world last year. This year I'm going somewhere else." But even that is no longer impossible. There have been a couple of "space tourists" willing to pay £13 or £14 million to go into space. Beyond my pocket, but I'd love to go myself. Maybe the next generation, or the one after that, will be partying on the planets.

Did you know that Jesus gave Christians an actual command to travel? *Go to all peoples everywhere and make them my disciples,* He said. That's how Christianity spread round the globe and why over a third of the world's population today is Christian – and rising. Some of the earliest Christians even struggled to the furthest, wettest, coldest, most pagan corner of the Roman Empire: England. Because God loved the world so much that He sent Jesus on a mission to save each of us. It was no holiday for Him.

---

[99] A Music Hall entertainer, who regularly performed on the radio programme "Workers' Playtime" in the 1950s.

SMART CARPENTERS

TUESDAY 30 JULY 2002

I love a good thunderstorm - so long as I'm safely indoors, in the dry. We had a good one yesterday evening, didn't we? All day it had been hot and humid. Then, the darkening clouds scudding towards us; the immense power of the lightning strokes; and the rumble and crack of the thunder. However clever we think we are, we haven't tamed the weather yet.

Two or three weeks ago, we were having three dozen friends round for a barbecue. And my wife put up our gazebo, just in case the weather turned bad. It didn't, but she wanted to be ready. I was summarily despatched to replace some of the tent pegs that had gone missing. And when the gazebo was up, it was firmly up, pegged down and guy-roped, as secure as she could make it. We've kept the gazebo up, and it's been pleasant to eat meals under its canopy, and even take an occasional chota-peg[100] in the balmy eventide.

Some neighbours were having a party of their own last Saturday, and they hastily put up a gazebo of their own. But not for them the guy ropes and the tent pegs. They just put it up and sat under it while they and their friends enjoyed themselves. But in yesterday's storm, their gazebo

---

[100] A relaxing drink, as practised in the days of the British Empire, particularly in India.

91

collapsed. It blew around their garden, scything down their flower beds and generally causing mayhem.

It reminded me of something Jesus said about the radical things He was teaching. Loving your neighbour, feeding the hungry, that sort of thing. And, perhaps even more radical: thinking evil is the same as doing evil.

He said *My words are not incidental additions to your life, DIY improvements to your living standards. If you work them into your life, you are like a smart carpenter who built his house on solid rock. Rain poured down, the river flooded, a tornado hit – but nothing moved that house. It was fixed to the rock. But if you just let my words pass you by and don't work them into your life, you're like a stupid carpenter who built his house on a sandy beach. When a storm rolled in and the waves came up, it collapsed like a house of cards*[101].

So smart carpenters don't rush to judge others. Smart carpenters give money to the Disasters Emergency Committee for the millions starving to death in Africa. Smart carpenters forgive those who hurt them. And smart carpenters know where they stand – on the foundations of the love of God.

---

[101] Matthew 7:24ff, my paraphrase.

COMMUNICATION

FRIDAY 13 SEPTEMBER 2002

Right now, as I speak to you, some of you are in your car, and maybe you're caught up in traffic, stop-starting your way to your destination. It's no comfort, but there was a humdinger of a hold-up on Saturday. The police, trying to deal with an incident involving a man on a bridge over the M1, closed down the local motorways. Thousands and thousands of people were caught up in an 18-mile, 8-hour tailback. I was trapped in a similar incident on the M6 myself once, and I know how frustrating it is to have to sit there waiting for an indefinite time. The greatest irritation is not knowing *why* you've been stopped for so long, and people have complained that the police didn't tell them why they'd had to close the motorways. I'm sure the police will be taking that on board in their review of the situation. The important thing, though, was that they ensured that no one was killed or injured in the incident.

Communication of information through language is one of the key things that distinguish mankind from the other animals. Following the agricultural age (when people stopped being hunter-gatherers and became farmers), and then the industrial age (when people stopped working on the land and started working in the manufacturing industries), we are now living in the communication age. There was the telegraph and the telex and the telephone, then radio and television. And quite recently we've had digital broadcasting and mobile phones and text messages and the internet. Who knows what is coming tomorrow?

Human communication is usually about rather more than passing on information, though. It is about creating and building relationships. There's a reader and a writer, a speaker and a listener, me and you, even.

Another distinguishing feature of the human species is the widespread need to communicate with God. Prayer is all about creating and building our relationship with God. Just like a child sitting on its parent's knee with the two of them talking. So when we pray, it's not to an impersonal force, but to a loving father (Jesus told us to call Him "Abba", which means "Dad") who wants the best for his children. And he always answers our prayers, though it's sometimes "Yes", sometimes "No" and sometimes "Not yet".

Which may help a little if you've just been praying, "God, get me out of this traffic jam"!

THE CHURCH AND HOMOSEXUALITY
THURSDAY 17 OCTOBER 2002

I don't often deal with real hot potatoes in this "Thought for the Day" slot. But there were some ill-considered statements on Thursday's "Talkback"[102] about the Christian view of homosexuality[103]. It was triggered off by the House of Lords vote to retain the bar on unmarried and gay couples adopting children. So, in a nutshell, what *does* the Church say?

First, it is abundantly clear that the Bible – the written word of God – in its few references to the subject, regards it as sinful. Sin is falling short of God's standards. God does not want *anyone* to sin sexually, whether through homosexual practice or adultery or fornication. The Christian believes the only acceptable place for *any* kind of sexual expression is within the bounds of the life-long, publicly declared, mutually avowed commitment we call marriage. Homosexual practice, whether by men or by women, is outside God's norms.

However, we must distinguish between homosexual inclination and homosexual practice. Homosexual preference is a desire. Homosexual practice is an action. Homosexual inclination is temptation. Homosexual practice is a yielding to that temptation. Here's good news: temptation is not sinful! It's how you deal with the temptation that matters.

---

[102] A Radio Leicester phone-in programme.
[103] I was telephoned by the producer and asked to speak on this subject, which I would have been unlikely to choose for myself.

What's the church's attitude towards those with a homosexual lifestyle? Christians are the first to acknowledge that we are all sinners. But we are *repentant* sinners, trying to live according to God's standards. Jesus said to those about to stone a woman for adultery: **The sinless one among you, go first: throw the stone[104]**. And one by one, the mob crept away, unable to comply. But then Jesus turned to the woman and said, **From now on, don't sin[105]**.

Christians are called to follow Jesus' example, loving people unconditionally. But, like Jesus, we have to confront sin, not condone it. Because homosexual practice is outside of God's intention for humankind, the church has to say that it is wrong to place needy adoptive children within a permanent homosexual lifestyle. It would be wrong to promote a homosexual lifestyle in schools. It *is* wrong to ordain unrepentant homosexual practitioners to the Christian ministry.

But hand-in-hand with this comes the love we have for those with a homosexual lifestyle. They are not inferior people. They are not to be hated, but valued and loved, just as Jesus values and loves us. We are all sinners, and we can all be forgiven.

---

[104] John 8:6 MSG
[105] John 8:11 MSG

REMEMBERING

FRIDAY 8 NOVEMBER 2002

It was my birthday this week. I'm not saying what birthday it was! Let's just say I was a post-war baby. Just. Oh, OK, work it out for yourself: On Wednesday I was 499,656 hours old. By comparison, good old BBC Radio Leicester isn't yet middle-aged, celebrating its 35th birthday today. That's a mere 306,816 hours! And during the course of today, we'll be looking back at all those hours of listening pleasure our favourite local station has brought us.

Looking back can bring painful memories as well as happy ones. 10th November this year is Remembrance Sunday. It's a day the nation recalls the men and women who fought for the good and important things now enshrined in the Universal Declaration of Human Rights. Things like the right to life, liberty and security of person; freedom from slavery, torture, from arbitrary arrest and imprisonment, and from oppressive interference with privacy; freedom to travel, to marry and have a family, freedom to own property, to assemble peacefully, to work, and to have our children educated. Things that the Nazi party denied to people under its rule. Things that we enjoy today, thanks to the heroism of previous generations.

Just what we remember depends on our own experiences. And those memories change and get clouded as time passes by. Distance *does* lend enchantment to the view. We tend to remember the happy times rather than the bad ones. Just as it hardly ever rained when we were children[106],

---

[106] Of course it didn t!

so many people's recollection of the 2nd World War concentrates on ITMA[107] and Workers' Playtime and Vera Lynn, forgetting the death and suffering and destruction the country was faced with, and the servicemen lived with, through five long years. And maybe this is a good thing, for bad memories can be very destructive.

There will be many tears shed this weekend as people remember their comrades in arms, their colleagues and friends, their relatives close and distant, who died and suffered in the conflicts this nation has endured. Let us not dwell on our sadness, but recall the good and positive memories.

Echoing St. Paul in his letter to the church at Philippi, we say, to all who made their sacrifice for our benefit, *I thank my God every time I remember you.*[108]

---

[107] **It's That Man Again**, an immensely popular BBC wireless comedy programme that ran from 1939 to 1949. It boosted "Home Front" morale during the dark war years. "That Man" of the title was Adolf Hitler.
[108] Philippians 1:3 NIVUK

IN FLANDERS FIELDS

In Flanders fields the poppies blow
Between the crosses, row on row,
That mark our place; and in the sky
The larks, still bravely singing, fly
Scarce heard amid the guns below.

       We are the Dead. Short days ago
       We lived, felt dawn, saw sunset glow,
       Loved and were loved, and now we lie
       In Flanders fields.

Take up our quarrel with the foe:
To you from failing hands we throw
The torch; be yours to hold it high.
If ye break faith with us who die
We shall not sleep, though poppies grow
In Flanders fields.

John McCrae
(1872 - 1918)

SANTA AND JESUS

FRIDAY 6 DECEMBER 2002

Today is celebrated as St Nicholas's Day. He's always been a popular saint, the patron saint of Russia and Greece and of children, sailors, scholars, and pawnbrokers. I don't know why he was connected with all of these, because not much is known about the life of this fourth century bishop. He is said to have left secret gifts of gold as dowries for three young women who would not have been able to marry otherwise. Some versions of the story say that he used to drop purses of coins down poor people's chimneys.

Perhaps that's why Saint Nicholas has become known to us by his abbreviated name of Santa Claus. Santa, who brings gifts to good little boys and girls. It wasn't until the late 1500s in England that gifts were given at Christmas-time rather than December 6th, as the reformers in the church put the emphasis on the Christ-child as the gift-giver on his own feast day, 25th December.

I've just come back from a holiday in Vienna, and in that beautiful city the windows of the sumptuous confectioners' shops are full of chocolate Santas – and, surprisingly, chocolate demons. In folk-lore from that part of Austria, a demon called Krampus is supposed to go around with Santa. Instead of bringing a sack, full of presents for good little children, Krampus brings a disappointing sackful of coal for the naughty ones. And the naughtiest of them all get carried away in Krampus's sack, never to be seen again.

Sounds like a good wheeze to make Viennese children behave themselves this time of year, anyway!

Santa, (who wears a scarlet costume) or Father Christmas (who wears a green costume) as we tend to call him in Britain, is a popular figure. He brings us presents, if we've been good.

But the Christian message is not quite the same. God gave the greatest gift of all, His son Jesus Christ, to an *undeserving* world. We haven't lived up to God's standards, yet everlasting and joyful life is *still* on offer to us. We haven't been well-behaved boys and girls, yet still He offers us the gifts of forgiveness and everlasting life. It's a gift for the asking.

So, forgetting your age: whether you've been a good little girl or boy, or a naughty one, you can still have your best Christmas present. And you don't have to wait until Christmas Day. But why not be a good little girl or boy anyway?

DETECTIVE CONSTABLE STEPHEN OAKE

MONDAY 20 JANUARY 2003

Yesterday at Poynton Baptist Church, there were two memorial services for Detective Constable Stephen Oake, who was killed on duty last week during an anti-terrorist enquiry sanctioned at the highest level of authority[109]. One service was for the public, and one for the church community itself. For Stephen Oake was an active member of that church, serving as a member of its governing body and as a lay preacher in the surrounding area.

The services sought to bring the shock of Stephen Oake's sudden death and lay it before the God of all comfort. They were also to mark the life of a man of integrity, to pay him tribute and also to thank God for his life. Stephen's parents, and his widow and children, committed Christians all, will have taken great consolation, not only in the support of their church, but of all churches who yesterday prayed for the family. Stephen's widow Lesley said they had been overwhelmed by messages of support from the public, from the Prime Minister, and from the Queen. Their greatest consolation, though, is the assurance, the Christian hope, that Stephen Oake rests in the loving arms of his Saviour, Jesus, where one day they will join him.

---

[109] Stephen Oake was stabbed by an al-Qaeda terrorist, Kamel Bourgass, who was resisting arrest. Bourgass was sentenced to life imprisonment, with a minimum tariff of 22 years. Other related offences added 15 and 17 years to his sentence. Stephen Oake was posthumously awarded the Queen's Gallantry Medal (awarded for "acts of exemplary bravery"), the third-ranking civilian gallantry medal after the George Cross and the George Medal.

I was struck by two statements made by those most closely affected by Stephen's death. First, his father, a former Chief Constable of the Isle of Man, said that he has been praying for God's forgiveness for the person who killed Stephen. That takes a real, solid Christian faith. To seek forgiveness for the killer of your child is something I can hardly imagine possible. Yet that is Stephen's father's prayer. And of course it is what Jesus asked for the Roman executioners as He was dying on the cross. "Father, forgive them," He said, "They don't know what they're doing." That must have been hard for our heavenly Father, but I have no doubt that those rough soldiers were forgiven at that instant.

The second thing was said by Lesley Oake, as she spoke about her husband. "Steve and I," she said, "Told each other every day that we loved each other". And Lesley Oake urged all married couples to do the same.

Isn't that good advice? Have you told your husband or your wife that you love him or her today? If you're still at home, why not do it right now? Or, as soon as you can, make a phone call to express your love. For as St Paul said, "Three things will last forever—faith, hope, and love—and the greatest of these is love[110]."

Just the three things that Stephen Oake epitomised.

Reverse of the Queen's Gallantry Medal

---

[110] 1 Corinthians 13:12 NLT

LOVE

I t's being pea-brained that causes it. Love, that is. The "pea" I'm referring to is phenylethylamine, known for short as "**P.E.A.**" It's a neurotransmitter, produced in your brain. And it interacts with other brain hormones to give you that heady, indescribable feeling of being in love. And today, there's going to be a lot of P.E.A. about, because it's St Valentine's Day.

Did *you* remember?

There are different kinds of love. The love that's in the air this St Valentine's Day is what the Greeks call *Eros*. It's the love between two unrelated people that leads to an attachment of the heart, and maybe on to marriage and children.

The Greeks also spoke of *Philos*, a "friendship" for someone or something. The Greek word pops up in words like *philosophy* – the love of knowledge. I guess there's *Filbertophiles* with a passion for Leicester City Football Club. Maybe they're going to become *Fossophiles* soon! This is the love for someone or something that leads to an attachment of the mind, and a deep interest and commitment to knowing all about the object of attention.

And there's a third word the Greeks used. It's the word *Agape*, and we don't have an exact equivalent in English. It expresses the highest, the most noble and devoted love that sees something unspeakably precious in the object of the love. It's the word that appears time and time again in the New Testament, describing God's love for all mankind and how God wants us to love each other. This is the love that leads to an attachment – a oneness - not only of your heart and mind, but of your will and your very being as well. It's the long-term love that grows and takes over when two people spend their lives together.

Jesus had a lot of hard things to say about love. It's easy to love your friends, but Jesus commands us - not *asks* us, but *commands* us - to love our enemies as well. And depending on Dr Blix's report to the United Nations later today, that might include Saddam Hussein as well. See how hard it is to live up to Jesus' commands?

But today, it's an easy one. It's our chance to express our *agape* love to that special someone with a card, with flowers, with chocolates, with a cosy candle-lit meal for two.

In a small way we're following God's example, after all: *This is how much God loved the world: He gave His Son, His one and only Son*[111].

---

[111] John 3:16 MSG

ALSO BY JOHN DENNEY

THE HISTORY OF
CHARTERED ACCOUNTANTS' BENEVOLENT
ASSOCIATION
1886-2011

172 pages, hardback.   ISBN 978-0-9567628-4-9

Available from the publishers,
CABA, 8 Mitchell Court, Castle Mound Way, Rugby, CV23 0UY
in return for a donation.

T he founding of the Chartered Accountants' Benevolent Association in 1886 marked the arrival of the Institute of Chartered Accountants in England and Wales as a fully fledged profession. From its beginning as an expression of Victorian philanthropy to its pioneering 21st Century innovations in the help it provides, the story of CABA's development is an absorbing one.

Through six monarchs, two world wars, 32 governments, a 130-fold expansion of ICAEW membership and the development of the Welfare State, CABA has not faltered in supporting Chartered Accountants and their dependants who have fallen on hard times.

A succession of remarkable men and women developed and administered CABA from its inception to the thriving organisation it is today. The generosity of a number of benefactors is noted, as is the growth of the endowed funds by dint of shrewd investment (and, in the earliest days, what we would now describe as "insider dealing").

The book includes

- many photographs and short biographies of some astonishing and entertaining people, including
    - some of the great names of the Accountancy profession: among them Arthur Cooper, Ernest Cooper, Sir William (WB) Peat, Sir Henry Peat, Sir John Sutherland Harmood-Banner, Edwin Waterhouse, William Welch Deloitte, and Frederick Whinney;
    - A notorious Lord Chief Justice who fathered illegitimate children and escaped from bailiffs by climbing out of a window;
    - A remarkable Woman of the Bedchamber to HM Queen Mary and daughter of the Master of Her Majesty's Buckhounds;
    - Winston Churchill's secretary, confidant and friend;
    - Lola Montez, an Irish courtesan, a German Countess, a Music Hall artiste and later a Methodist worker in New York;
- notes on the appalling misery of the poor in Victorian Britain, in prison and workhouse, including a description of the unspeakable "less eligibility" principle and its consequences;
- insights into the practices and costs of funerals in Victorian times;
- John's translation of a Dutch humorous poem, *De Leeuw* (The Lion) by Gerrit van de Linde, the Dutch Poet Laureate.

This book is for everyone, not just Chartered Accountants.

RESPECT AND CONSIDERATION
BRITAIN IN JAPAN 1853 - 1868 AND BEYOND
How Britain helped Japan move from feudalism
to join the modern community of nations
生麦事件
Through mendacity mayhem and murder
via the Richardson Affair
to the Meiji Restoration
明治維新

528 pages, paperback   ISBN 978-0-9568798-0-6

Radiance Press

Available from Amazon, other internet sellers and bookshops.   £21.99

This book recounts the little-remembered part that Britain and the West played in the momentous events in Japan between 1853 and 1868. In just fifteen years, a repressive feudal règime was transformed into an embryonic democracy under the broadly benevolent eye of the young Emperor Meiji. Over 260 years of rigid rule by hereditary Tokugawa *shōguns* was swept aside, with trade as a mainspring of revolution. But the transition was punctuated with dissent and deceit, murder and mayhem. The backwoodsmen among the *samurai* would not be displaced without a fight. And they got one, from the Royal Navy, supported by other Western naval and military forces.

The archives and the public and private accounts left

by eye witnesses record the story revealed in *Respect and Consideration*. The multiple backgrounds – mythological, cultural, religious, historical, geographic, naval, military, diplomatic – are painted in. Over 200 photographs and illustrations show the people and the places. Biographies of over 50 of the key people - Japanese and Western) who influenced the course of events are given. The events are thoroughly detailed. Their consequences are set out. 6 maps and 19 tables give detailed information.

Centring on the murder of a young English merchant from Shanghai passing through Japan on his way home to rejoin his family in Croydon one warm Sunday afternoon in 1862, the book draws together the threads that led to the brutal act, and what consequences flowed from it. This was perhaps the final flourish of full-blooded gunboat diplomacy.

Respect and Consideration will fascinate you, inform you, horrify you and entertain you. You will be drawn into the heady ferment of the *bakumatsu*, when Japan was thrust, willy-nilly, into the modern world. And you will see how this was not one-way traffic: see how the culture and diplomacy of the West was influenced by Japan.

A sample from *Respect and Consideration* starts on the following page

INTRODUCTION

I n the International Cemetery in Yokohama lie the graves of three Englishmen, side by side. Two died peacefully in their beds. The faint epitaph on the central tombstone reads:

> **SACRED**
> TO THE MEMORY OF
> **C. L. RICHARDSON**
> LATE OF SHANGHAI
> AGED 28 YEARS
> WHO WAS
> CRUELLY ASSASSINATED
> BY JAPANESE
> ON THE TOCAIDO
> NEAR KANAGAWA
> SEP 14 1862

In a nutshell, the three Englishmen and a young woman were out for a ride near Yokohama. They stumbled into a procession that was taking the *daimyō* (Lord) of Satsuma, one of the most important Japanese nobles, from the *shōgun's* palace in Edo (now Tōkyō) to the Emperor's palace in Kyōto. His bodyguards drew their swords and laid into the four riders. Three escaped, two of them gravely wounded, but the fourth received fatal injuries.

The British government demanded compensation from the Japanese government and from the *daimyō* concerned. They also demanded that the perpetrators of the murder be caught, tried and executed.

The Japanese Government paid up; the *daimyō* refused. So, the following year, the Royal Navy approached Kagoshima, capital of the Satsuma domain. To coerce the Lord of Satsuma to comply with British demands, the Royal Navy seized three of his ships; there was an exchange of gunfire; there was loss of life on both sides; a large part of the town was burned down; both sides claimed a victory.

In parallel, the *daimyō* of Chōshū waged a private war against the westerners in Japan, so the naval and military forces of five

110

nations, under British command, responded robustly. Subsequently, the Lords of Satsuma and Chōshū negotiated settlements with the British; compensation was paid, and friendly commercial relations gradually prevailed, with a supplementary handful of western casualties in the cause of *rapprochement*. Japan came out from its hundreds of years of feudal seclusion and joined the prosperous democracies of the West.

But how did this astonishing story come about? Why was that particular Englishman to die by *samurai* sword on that Sunday afternoon? What historical forces were behind the events? What actually happened that Sunday afternoon? What was the reaction of the small foreign community in Yokohama? What relationship was there between the naval engagements at Kagoshima and Shimonoseki? And what were the consequences of these events?

This account is an attempt to answer these questions and to look at some aspects of Anglo-Japanese relationships during the *bakumatsu*, the fifteen years from 1853 to 1868 - and beyond. The paradigm shift that swept Japan from an introspective, exclusivist, feudal dictatorship to an outgoing western-style trading democracy in fifteen years was unprecedented.

The murder of Charles Richardson and its consequences outlined above does much to shed light on the turbulent events in Japan at the time, and on the Western governments' - particularly the British government's - attitudes towards Japan, in an era when Britain truly ruled the waves. This is as much a story about the era of gunboat diplomacy as about the end of 700 years of a system of Japanese government. The legacy of these events still reverberates in Japanese society today.

And all of this took place in the days before telegraphic communication facilitated contact between the representatives in foreign lands and their government in London. A request from the British Minister Plenipotentiary in Japan for instructions from the Foreign Secretary nearly 10,000 miles away might receive a reply as much as four months later. Thus this was the last period in which the British Minister required truly plenipotentiary powers, for he had to take his own decisions within the general brief he carried. The Minister was always anxious to hear of his government's approval of his actions.

It has proved impossible to retain a strict chronological sequence in this history if we are to make sense of events. If you skip straight to Chapter 11, you'll get the excitement of the events, but won't understand what led up to them, so do start at Chapter 1!

I do not apologise for frequent digressions into secondary areas that I hope the reader will find as curious, informative and entertaining as I do. They fill in the background and explain some of what occurred. Where possible, I have included these things in the main text, but others have to remain as footnotes, or else the narrative would become too complex. But if I have appeared to be applying to enter the ancient Chinese Civil Service, where candidates were locked in a room for three days and two nights and told to write down everything they knew, then that is the way it is. So many threads intertwine in the rich tapestry we call "history". I have had to be selective in what I have included; else this would have been a multi-volume work. It has felt at times as if I were trying to pour a quart into a thimble.

I hope this book may serve as an introduction to Japanese thought, history and culture, as an insight into the workings of the Royal Navy, as a remembrance of one of the last uses of gunboat diplomacy, as a record of the successful use of patient diplomacy, and as a reminder of a remarkable period in history, largely neglected, forgotten or ignored, especially in the West.

I trust you find this journey into the ferment of the *bakumatsu* as interesting and rewarding as I have done.

www.ingramcontent.com/pod-product-compliance
Lightning Source LLC
LaVergne TN
LVHW090047090426
835511LV00031B/372